Bold is Idealism.

Bold is Vision.

Bold is Risk.

Bold is Impact.

bold

Create a **career** with impact.

By Cheryl L. Dorsey and Lara Galinsky

Echoing Green
Email: bebold@echoinggreen.org
Tel: 212.689.1165

First Edition

Photography Credits:

Cover and page 10 photograph of a diver: George Kavanagh / Stone + / Getty Images
Pages 14 and 16: Photographs of David Lewis, copyright Ken Paul Rosenthal
Page 20: Photograph of Priya Haji, copyright Daniel Lorenze
Page 26: Photograph of Kyra Bobinet, copyright Ken Paul Rosenthal
Page 32: Photograph of Karen Tse, copyright John Emerson
Page 34: Photograph of Karen Tse, copyright Sean MacLeod
Page 41: Photograph of Wendy Kopp, copyright Jean-Christian Bourcart
Page 47: Photograph of Michael Brown, copyright Jim Harrison
Page 54: Photograph of Eric Rosenthal, copyright Lloyd Wolf
Page 56: Photograph of Eric Rosenthal in a Romanian psychiatric institution, used with the permission from MDRI, copyright Richard Mertens
Page 62: Photograph of Eric Adler, copyright Lloyd Wolf
Page 67: Photograph of Rajiv Vinnakota, copyright Lloyd Wolf
Page 70: Photograph of Eric Adler and Rajiv Vinnakota, copyright Lloyd Wolf
Page 73: Photograph of City Year corps members, used with the permission from City Year, copyright Jennifer D. Cogswell
Pages 74 and 76: Photographs of Katie Redford, copyright Lloyd Wolf
Page 82: Photograph of Carolyn Laub, copyright Ken Paul Rosenthal
Page 86: Photograph of Maya Ajmera, used with the permission from The Global Fund for Children
Page 92: Photograph of students, used with the permission from Teach For America, copyright Jean-Christian Bourcart

Printed in Canada

Being bold is being environmentally-friendly. Therefore, *Be Bold* is printed on recycled paper.

Contents

Acknowledgments

This book has been in the making for twenty years. Since 1987, Echoing Green has had the privilege of working with some of the best young leaders of their generation. Their stories deserved to be told and shared with others seeking to make a positive impact on the world. We are grateful to the Echoing Green Fellows featured in *Be Bold* for opening up about their dreams, triumphs, and challenges; we are equally grateful to the hundreds of other Echoing Green Fellows who inspire us every day and have built an unbreakable community of hope and action.

Be Bold would not have been possible without the leadership, support, and good humor of Dan Weiss, Echoing Green Board Member and Publisher and Managing Director of Spark Publishing. He guided us through every step of this journey and graciously introduced us to the talented people on the Spark Publishing team. Thank you for teaching us about the joys and deadlines (!) that come with publishing our own book and being an amazing champion for this project every step of the way.

Thank you as well to the volunteer Spark Publishing team pros for providing us with your valuable guidance and feedback:

Margo Orlando, who was with us from the beginning, interviewing the fellows and shaping their stories; Liz Kessler, Laurie Barnett, and Susan D'Orazio, whose superb management and editorial skills helped us stay on track and say what we wanted to say in a clear, concise manner; Daniel O. Williams, Frances Duncan, and Loira Walsh, talented designers who created a beautiful and bold look for the book and website, perfectly matching the power of the words with the power of the images; and Tammy Hepps and Melissa Camero, our tech developers who helped create a dynamic website, www.bebold.org, to bring *Be Bold*'s ideas to a wider audience, hopefully, over the next few years.

If it takes a village to raise a child, then it certainly took one to bring *Be Bold* to fruition. So many friends and supporters shared the "three t's"—time, talent, and treasure—to bring the message of *Be Bold* to the widest possible audience. First and foremost, we are deeply grateful to our anchor partners—organizations and companies that have committed to promote and support the *Be Bold* initiative comprehensively. It has been a pleasure to work with Michael Brown, Andrea Eaton, and Alison Franklin at City Year; Ben Goldhirsh, Audrey Desiderato, Tara McConaghy, and Max Schorr at GOOD Magazine; Kala Stroup, Shelly Cryer, and Patrick Sallee at American Humanics; Russ

Finkelstein at Idealist; Tom Reis at the W.K. Kellogg Foundation; and Chris Hadley, Ira Silberstein, and Shivani York at *The New York Times*. Also, thank you to our many distribution partners who are leveraging their networks—both wide and deep—to get *Be Bold* into the hands of as many readers as possible. Too numerous to name here, they are all listed in the resources section of the book.

We also are grateful to friends such as David Bornstein, Raphael Bemporad, Mitch Baranowski, Paul Light, Meredith Blake, Billy Shore, and Gregg Petersmeyer, who gave us encouragement and important advice along the way. Expert guidance on book distribution came from our key advisors—Suzanne Muchin and Halee Sage-Friedman. We thank Michael Vagnetti for his much needed book fulfillment assistance and Dot Lin for her editorial skills. Alison King, Christopher R. Brewster, Jesse M. Brody, Jeremy White, Alan L. Friel, and Kerren R. Misulovin, attorneys at Kaye Scholer LLP., offered us superb legal counsel. Rene Jones of the UTA Foundation, Bridgit Evans from Live for Darfur, Mark Hanis from Genocide Intervention Network, Sasha Chanoff from Mapendo International, and Lenore Zerman of Liberman/Zerman connected us to Don Cheadle and John Prendergast. Actor and activist, these two luminaries set the tone for the book with an important call to action. And what would we have done without the generous financial support we received from those who saw the promise of *Be Bold* and deeply believe in building the next generation of nonprofit leaders? Thank you to James and Gretchen Rubin, Roland and Mary DeSilva, Michael Loeb, Linetta Gilbert of the Ford Foundation, and, again, Tom Reis of the W. K. Kellogg Foundation and Dan Weiss.

Finally, we offer a heartfelt thank you to current and former Echoing Green staff members who took to the project with customary fearlessness and dedication. Leslie Liao, Shahnaz Habib, and Leena Soman worked tirelessly to ensure that the initiative ran smoothly. As befits an effort that promotes the power of young people, our interns—Analia Bongiovani, Dave Lewis, Sughosh Venkatesh, Zachary Potter Vose, Sara Weiss, and Eli Wolfe—all provided key support and input over the course of the initiative. We humbly ask the forgiveness of anyone we may have overlooked. Please know how grateful we are to one and all who helped make *Be Bold* a reality; we are simply overwhelmed by the bounty, grace, and goodwill of all those who believe in the initiative as much as we do.

October 2006

Dear Reader:

You may have seen *Hotel Rwanda* or heard its story. If you have, then you know of Paul Rusesabagina. It was his individual act of heroism that saved over 1,200 lives during the Rwandan genocide, in which over 800,000 human beings were killed in 100 days. Paul is boldness personified. The film is a reminder of what can happen when good men and women stand by and *do nothing*; it also demonstrates what grace looks like—how one person standing up can make a difference. All of us are potential *upstanders* if we so choose.

Mr. Cheadle was nominated for an Academy Award for his performance in the film *Hotel Rwanda* and helped produce and appeared in the Oscar-winning film *Crash*. Mr. Prendergast is a senior adviser to the International Crisis Group (www.crisisgroup.org) and worked for President Clinton's National Security Council. They are working on a book on citizen action, to be published in Spring 2007 by Hyperion.

In January 2005, we went to Darfur, in the western region of Sudan, where state-sponsored genocide and brutality has resulted in 400,000 civilian deaths and displaced over 2.5 million people. Looking into the eyes of and talking with refugees from Darfur who were terrified, homeless, hungry, and innocent, we knew more had to be done. And quickly. We had to take a stand...again. We have banded together, tapping into our collective power to speak truth to power and to raise awareness about these atrocities. In addition to Darfur, we also went to Northern Uganda, conducted speeches, wrote op-eds, attended rallies, convened meetings of influentials, and visited members of Congress. We are proud to stand shoulder to shoulder with thousands of others around the world who also are fighting to end the genocide in Darfur. There is so much more to be done. The world needs more people to be bold and take on this important work for our tomorrow.

Never forget that doing *nothing* is as much a choice as doing *something*. Choosing to get engaged in a cause that you deeply care about or launching a career in the nonprofit sector are not only courageous acts of service, but also the most powerful weapon against the horrors and injustices of the world that require indifference, inaction, and silence to thrive. For those working in the nonprofit sector or considering a nonprofit career, your fulltime commitment to working on the social problems of our time is truly commendable. Your skills, energy, and passion are very much needed and appreciated.

Be Bold will be an indispensable guide as your journey of service continues. It will help you to understand what drives you and where your talents are needed. It will ask you to look critically at the problems in your community and identify the barriers to progress. It will encourage you to craft your vision of positive social change as well as your role in achieving it. Most of all, *Be Bold* will help you recognize your own power to change the world. This is an awesome realization.

Accept it, embrace it, and get started.

Sincerely,

Don Cheadle and **John Prendergast**

Introduction

Why Be Bold?

The urge to live a life of meaning is one of our most elemental desires as human beings. We *want* to make a difference in the world; we *need* to leave our footprint in the sands of time to mark our existence. By honoring the beliefs and values we hold dear, we allow ourselves to live lives that matter.

This includes decisions about your career, because your career is more than just a job. It is a way of leaving your footprint. To find a career that matters to you—truly matters—you must first know and understand yourself. This means examining your strengths and weaknesses, acknowledging your fears, and letting go of everyone else's expectations except your own. It means discovering your truest self and fiercely protecting that discovery. You can learn about yourself by being open to a variety of experiences, including academic courses, volunteer work, hobbies, jobs, and cultural ventures, such as traveling or living abroad. Pay attention to what feels right and what doesn't. Learn as much from the negative experiences as the positive ones. By committing to the process of really getting to know yourself, you can reach unbelievable heights in life and find a career that is perfect for you.

A meaningful life will mean something different for everyone. It may mean following a lucrative career track in the for-profit world, it may mean pursuing athletic or artistic talents, or it may mean being a terrific parent.

For many, a career of service is the path to a meaningful life. *Be Bold* is written for those of you who are considering or already pursuing a career in the nonprofit sector. It celebrates your choice and helps you explore your link to this dynamic industry.

A career in the nonprofit sector offers tremendous benefits. First and foremost, it offers you the opportunity to serve society professionally. Whether you are working for a nonprofit organization that addresses community needs or for one that advocates for community and social changes, you are adding your voice and devoting your talents to a sector that collectively cares for the needs of many, including the most severely disadvantaged, and challenges societies to live up to their highest ideals. The nonprofit sector is also remarkably diverse, offering something for everyone. It allows you to do interesting work in a variety of settings, take on an array of public issues and problems, and

receive valuable exposure to different types of people.

For the past twenty years, Echoing Green (**www.echoinggreen.org**) has had the privilege of working with some of the most promising emerging leaders in the nonprofit sector. Through our prestigious fellowship program, we have supported over 400 visionary individuals around the world in their efforts to create bold, groundbreaking nonprofit organizations: new schools for low-income students, advocacy organizations that speak truth to power, effective arts education programs, large-scale public service projects, health-care programs for the needy, innovative legal services programs for the marginalized, and many more. We have watched in awe as Echoing Green Fellows have translated personal excellence, passion, and dedication into careers that have a tremendous impact on the world.

In *Be Bold*, we share the stories of twelve Echoing Green Fellows. These nonprofit leaders are changing their communities, their nations, and the world for the better. We hope that in their stories you will recognize part of your own journey and find inspiration. We believe wholeheartedly that you, too, have the power to change the world if you choose to accept this responsibility. It requires you to make the decision to live and act boldly and then stand firm in that choice. This is our call to action. We are asking you to **Be Bold**.

Be Bold outlines four core elements that will help you be bold in your life and in your career in the nonprofit sector:

- **Moment of Obligation:** identifying what means the most to you and committing to carrying out your dreams

- **Gall to Think Big:** believing you can take on the world and developing a clear and expansive vision for change

- **New and Untested:** questioning the status quo and creating new solutions to address seemingly intractable social problems

- **Seeing Possibilities:** identifying solutions when others can't and having hope when others don't

It is our wish that you will use Be Bold as a guide, a workbook, and a plan for change. Turning the page begins a new chapter in the way you think about your life and career. Find the courage to **Be Bold**. New possibilities await.

David Lewis, *Echoing Green Fellow, in front of San Quentin prison*

Chapter 1

Moment of Obligation

What Is a *Moment of Obligation?*

At certain moments in your life, you may find yourself pulled toward a path leading to work that will benefit others. If you seize these moments—if you make a bold decision to take action—a different world—a *better* world—is within reach. Some people can pinpoint one particular moment during which their lives took a new turn. Other people experience a *series* of moments that build upon one another. The key is to turn these moments of opportunity into concrete action.

Whether your goal is to start a nonprofit organization, involve yourself in one, or simply learn more about careers in the sector, you will reach a point at which your thoughts, plans, discussions, and experiences teeter on the brink of turning into action. You will have the choice to move forward or to do nothing. Making a sincere commitment to act is a *moment of obligation*. When you seize a *moment of obligation*, you accept responsibility for your dreams and gather the courage to follow a path no matter where it leads. The obligation is actually to yourself—to pursue what means the most to you.

According to a recent study by Paul Light of the Brookings Institution, 62 percent of graduating college seniors are interested in careers related to public service, yet only 9 percent know a great deal on how to go about finding a job in the nonprofit sector (Shelly Cryer, "Recruiting and Retaining the Next Generation of Nonprofit Sector Leadership," The Initiative for Nonprofit Sector Careers, 2004). With more than 12.5 million people working in nonprofit organizations in the United States—that's 9.5 percent of the country's workforce—the nonprofit sector is growing at a faster rate than the government and private sectors. Thus, there are many ways to gain exposure to new things, yet you must be open to these experiences because true boldness emerges when you gather these moments, decipher them, trust in their significance, and follow them toward your *moment of obligation*.

The Path Isn't Always Straight

By age fifteen, David Lewis was a full-blown heroin addict, holding up minimarts, selling drugs, and stealing people's things—doing whatever was necessary to feed his habit in drug-ridden East Palo Alto, California. A high-school dropout, David believed that dealing drugs was his only option for survival. At age nineteen, he was arrested for selling heroin and sentenced to ten years to life in prison.

The day that David arrived at San Quentin, California's oldest and most notorious correctional institution, an officer told him that he was one of the youngest people there. If David "acted like a man," the officer said, he would be okay—but if he "played kid games," he would get into trouble and possibly get himself killed. The words stuck with David. He started looking for allies and men to whom he could relate. He fell in with one of the most dangerous gangs in the prison system and quickly picked up its strategies for surviving and gaining status. So skilled was he at extortion, ransom, and drug dealing that eventually he coordinated most of the illegal activities in San Quentin. David's entrepreneurial gifts, wit, strategic thinking, and charisma gave him immense influence over other prisoners. It was these same qualities that would one day enable him to become a force for good in his community.

David's first *moment of obligation* occurred two months before his release in 1989, when the Loma Prieta earthquake rocked California. Trapped in his trembling cell in the fifth tier of San Quentin, he faced the horrific possibility of dying alone. David was overcome with a deep sadness about his situation. For the first time, the prospect of a different life seemed more appealing than the one he had always known. A new vision for his future was sparked. David began to see the end of his prison term as a chance to play a meaningful role in society.

When David was released at age thirty-four, he returned to East Palo Alto, determined to start over. But the familiar temptations of dealers and drugs quickly surrounded him. He had no housing, no job, and no traditional life skills. David fell back into his old habits. Like almost 70 percent of released prisoners, he was rearrested within three years.

Being Bold means taking responsibilty for your dreams.

Instead of sending him back to prison, David's parole officer enrolled him in a year-long residential drug treatment center in East Palo Alto. At the center, David's desire to improve himself took root. He formed a group called the Circle of Recovery. Members of the group, who were trying to stay clean and sober, shared their experiences and fears and supported one another. The Circle, which had a remarkable impact on its

"Even in prison, even when I was a drug addict, I have always been a person who was able to venture outside the nine dots of traditional methods."

—David Lewis

members, was featured in a 1991 PBS documentary hosted by Bill Moyers. As a member of the Circle, David finally came to terms with the harm his addiction had caused to others, particularly the sons he hadn't raised. As the founder of the Circle, David realized that the widely accepted model for helping substance abusers, which involved taking people out of their communities to recover, was not always the most effective strategy. He came to believe that addicts' own communities, as a loving and supportive force, could—and should—help them.

By 1992, East Palo Alto had become the "murder capital" of the United States. In an effort to lower the homicide rate, local leaders enlisted the help of the FBI and the police force, a strategy that caused a lot of tension in the community. David opposed these tactics. His own recovery process had shown him that solutions from within the community proved more effective than solutions imposed from the outside. The mayor of East Palo Alto, who had seen the Moyers documentary, asked to meet with David. She wanted him to help solve the problems of East Palo Alto by using the kind of community-based recovery models the Circle relied on.

A moment of obligation is the discovery of exactly what inspires you.

David's triumph over drugs paved the way for his second *moment of obligation*. He wanted to extend his victory to others, enact his ideas about community-based recovery programs, and pursue improvements in the field of recovery. His struggle to stay clean and reintegrate into society after his prison release showed him how many gaps existed in current treatment structures. East Palo Alto provided many different services for those in need, including violence prevention, substance abuse support, and public health programs. But the groups did not communicate with one another, and no group used a holistic approach. David was convinced that the best approach to treatment involved providing the entire spectrum of services—housing, jobs, transportation, and support—under one roof, right inside the community. He believed that making the community the focal point for recovery would help lower the crime rate.

Responding to a moment of obligation means applying your beliefs, skills, and experiences to build a better world.

When David shared his ideas with the mayor and others in the community, they were interested. The old approach resulted in violence and a high crime rate, so why not attempt a new solution? David collaborated with two like-minded change agents: Priya Haji, a Stanford University student, and Vicki Smothers, a community activist from East Palo Alto. In 1993, they launched Free at Last, an East Palo Alto–based service to help recovering addicts. Its motto is "In the community, by the community, for the community," and its mission is to provide drug intervention and prevention services to local residents, with a special focus on those affected by incarceration, HIV/AIDS, and intergenerational addiction.

Instead of following traditional recovery models, Free at Last operates locally and is staffed by community members. Sixty-five percent of the group's staff members are in recovery, 85 percent are local residents, and many are former clients of the program. Free at Last provides a wide array of services, including bilingual twelve-step programs for substance-abuse treatment, job placement services, transitional housing, HIV prevention and education, and social support.

During the first year of Free at Last's existence, the crime rate in East Palo Alto dropped by 87 percent. Now, over a decade later, the organization has served more than 30,000 clients and has been a powerful source of change in the community. A recent study found that of all the participants who completed the program, more than 70 percent were still clean and sober, off public assistance and employed, and living in independent housing where they were responsible for paying their bills. The group continues to thrive, and its model is being expanded internationally—from Massachusetts to Kenya. David travels around the world over 100 days a year to speak about his organization and its proven model for recovery. In recognition of his accomplishments, David was awarded the California Peace Prize in 1994.

Responding to a moment of obligation means recognizing your ability to make a unique contribution and finding the strength to take the first step.

David managed to turn around his own life as well as the lives of thousands of others. He says he achieved these feats by relying on "intestinal fortitude." He knows that his seventeen years in prison played a key role in helping him develop that strength. "I did a lot of inventory on myself, a lot of soul searching. I was born for my *moments of obligation*. The adversities I went through were preparation for the work I was born to do," he says.

"Once we started Free at Last, the word started to spread throughout the community and the prisons that people could come back to the community and find some healing. Healing provided by people who looked like them, smelled like them. Were them."

—David Lewis

David believes that everyone is imprisoned in some way—by bad habits, inertia, lack of confidence, and so on—and that people can use their difficult experiences as preparation for facing *moments of obligation*. Taking a hard look at yourself, asking difficult questions, and committing to the service of others requires building intestinal fortitude. When we recognize *moments of obligation*, we must tap into this strength.

Hardwired for Service

East Palo Alto is just five miles away from Stanford University, but in 1992, the city's violent, drug-ridden corners seemed worlds away from the campus' hallowed halls. Priya Haji straddled both worlds: as an HIV prevention volunteer, she handed out bleach and condoms on the streets of East Palo Alto; as a senior at Stanford University, she was a religious studies major and a premed student.

Being Bold is moving outside of your comfort zone.

Priya's family background primed her for service. Her grandparents had been social activists in India and East Africa, and her parents had instilled in her a sense of social responsibility. By age sixteen, she had experienced her first in a series of *moments of obligation*. She helped her father, a surgeon, set up a free health clinic in the small Texas town in which her family lived—clinic that eventually grew to include Priya's mother, a family practitioner, as well as many other volunteers. Hardwired for service, Priya took advantage of many opportunities to make a difference. She volunteered throughout high school and college, doing work that eventually led her to forge a partnership with David Lewis.

Priya's commitment to the nonprofit sector is inspired both by her beliefs and by her triumph over her own personal challenges. Growing up in a small town in Texas with Indian-immigrant physician parents, Priya was always encouraged to focus on academics and excel in extra-curricular activities like sports and student government. Even though on the outside things always seemed fine, like many teenage girls, she was struggling on the inside because she had faced molestation and kept it a secret. As her inner turmoil manifested negatively in her early twenties, Priya decided to take a year off from college to work through things. With the support of many friends and family, she began

to sort things out—it was at that time she made a commitment to focusing her own energy on helping women from less fortunate circumstances who were facing challenges similar to what she had experienced and overcome.

Enacting a moment of obligation means embracing social responsibility.

Priya's commitment to social change came into focus one day in 1992. She was handing out condoms on an East Palo Alto street corner when a man pulled up in a gray pickup truck and asked, "What do you think you're doing?" This man, clad in baggy overalls and sporting an impressive handlebar mustache, turned out to be David Lewis. Priya confidently stated that she wanted to reduce STD infection rates in East Palo Alto. For over an hour, Priya, with HIV-prevention materials still in hand, and David, head sticking out of the window of his truck, engaged in a heated discussion. Priya found David charismatic, complex, and inspiring, and David, who was accustomed to people being intimidated by him, was intrigued by Priya's spunk.

David invited Priya to get involved with his new idea for community recovery. She started accompanying him on weekly trips to San Quentin, the prison where he had been incarcerated for seventeen years. Priya says, "Every day, I would hop on the bus or my bike, go to East Palo Alto, and meet David wherever he was. If he was doing a counseling group, I'd pass out the sign-in sheet, or I'd organize the files. I was just around." She was outraged by the injustice she witnessed in the minority-dominated prison system and by the fact that prisoners were given very little support or training before reentering society. She shared David's beliefs that prison terms were not the best way to help addicts and that most people in recovery had few or no resources to rely on when released.

During their trips to the prison and around East Palo Alto, Priya and David talked about what kind of organization could best help addicts in the community. Along with Vicki Smothers, Priya helped build a women's health education program, while with David, she worked on a prison outreach program. Although the work moved forward in increments, a powerful vision of community-based treatment started to take shape.

When Priya spotted a flyer in her dorm detailing the Echoing Green Fellowship program, which would provide valuable seed funding for innovative ideas that furthered social change, her resolve to build an organization with David crystallized. With David and Vicki, she wrote an organizational plan and successfully applied for the fellowship. Priya became the first executive director of Free at Last.

Priya's *moment of obligation* to start Free at Last with David and Vicki led her to discover one of her strengths: the ability to see what she calls "a vision beyond reality"—a new reality that does not yet exist but that she can clearly imagine. At such a young age, Priya did not know what her full capabilities were, yet she went forward nonetheless. She fulfilled the call of her *moment of obligation*. Who would have imagined that two people with such different backgrounds and experiences would come together in a common cause and ignite a movement that has changed the lives of tens of thousands, catalyzed much-needed improvements in a community, and become a model for recovery programs everywhere?

"How we use our privileges and opportunities defines what kind of person we are."
—Priya Haji

Although Priya was appointed the executive director of Free at Last, she was, in many ways, a disciple of David and Vicki, whose experiences and knowledge exceeded her own. She needed to learn the basics before she could work toward a larger vision. She accompanied David and Vicki to different recovery programs and transitional houses, she referred clients to appropriate programs and then followed them there to observe the way those programs functioned, and she worked in the trenches every day at Free at Last, helping clients and learning technical details from David. "Eighty percent of my learning was from David and Vicki," she says. Priya believes that all great leaders must first be great apprentices. She has seen many intelligent young people make the false assumption that they must emerge instantly as leaders. True boldness involves a willingness to learn from others.

Fulfilling a moment of obligation sometimes means being an apprentice first.

With each passing year, Priya gained more skills and Free at Last met the community's needs more successfully. During Priya's seven years as executive director, the organization exceeded each one of its initial goals. What began as a storefront operation that employed two people and shared a pay phone with drug dealers eventually evolved into an organization with a budget of well over $1 million, ten facilities, and more than 4,000 clients a year. In 1998, Priya was named one of America's Ten Most Outstanding Young Leaders by Do Something, MTV, and *Mademoiselle* magazine.

In 2000, Priya faced her next *moment of obligation*. After many calls home and much soul searching and late-night journal writing, she decided that it was time to move on from Free at Last. She had realized that the organization did not need to keep growing but, rather, needed to maintain its effectiveness and codify its programs. She believed that others were better suited to lead the organization in this new direction, and she felt compelled to draw on her own particular talent for creating something new. This time, she thought she might want to create a hybrid for-profit/nonprofit organization that could make business itself a vehicle for social change. The following fall, Priya enrolled in the University of California's MBA program at Berkeley's Haas School of Business to develop some of the skills to take on this new challenge.

"If you're a successful entrepreneur, you see something that's not real, but you believe in it so deeply and can paint it so vividly, and your conviction is so deep, that other people can see it through you."

—Priya Haji

In business school, Priya looked at problems that could be solved by aligning social causes with the power of the business marketplace. She was interested in working on something with infinite scalability, as well as on issues connected to women of color. These interests became linked during her study of fair trade, a field that focuses mainly on agricultural commodities over the past decade. Priya wanted to extend the framework of fair trade to include the goods of global artisan communities.

Responding to a moment of obligation means identifying the intersection between talent and passion.

After graduating from business school, Priya spent six months traveling through Latin America and Asia. In cities and villages in every country, she found artisans who had set up nonprofits and small cooperatives to produce and sell their wares. Recognizing the beginning of a *moment of obligation*, she looked at women who were knitting or weaving and saw herself. *I could have been them; they could have been me,* she thought. These women were different from her only because of the "accident of birth." Priya felt so connected to them that she considered moving to one of the countries she visited and designing handicrafts herself.

However, she discovered that her business education gave her a way to be of greater use. Many artisans said that they needed help breaking into the growing crafts market in the United States. Priya knew she could aid in this effort. Many Americans settle for machine-made versions of artisan items because they do not travel internationally and thus cannot purchase these items firsthand. Priya wanted to help the women capitalize on the American interest in artisan goods and do so in a way that could be replicated to help thousands of other artisans around the world.

In 2003, with Siddharth Sanghvi, Priya co-founded World of Good to create U.S. market demand for international artisan products. A for-profit/nonprofit social enterprise, her new organization promotes fair trade and economic growth for artisans products in Asia, Africa, and Latin America by making their goods widely available to American consumers. Today, World of Good products are displayed in popular retail outlets nationwide such as Whole Foods, Wild Oats, Follett Campus Bookstores, and many other independent retailers committed to selling fair trade products. Ten percent of the profits go to World of Good's nonprofit arm, World of Good Development Organization, which supports economic development in artisan communities. With a focus on strengthening industry standards, the Development Organization has built a revolutionary web-based tool called the Fair Trade Wage Guide that allows artisans and traders anywhere in the world to calculate a fair price for their product.

Priya's new organization is the product of her talents and her steadfast commitment to tackling tough social problems. Her passion for social change is not limited to one particular field. Since personal interests and social problems constantly evolve, she may one day leave World of Good and commit herself to another initiative. A self-described "serial social entrepreneur" with a deep connection to many issues, Priya likely will turn her entrepreneurial spirit toward new challenges. David and Priya's paths both make clear that *moments of obligation* are rooted in different interests and sparked by different experiences, but that all are the ultimate expressions of your internal compass—that is your sense of purpose.

"I believe people are compelled to do certain work—they have the most powerful, present sense of themselves. They're on fire because they're doing what they're supposed to be doing."
—Priya Haji

and served on multiple medical school leadership committees.

Being Bold is embracing unexpected change.

But at 3 a.m. one morning, wide awake after fending off another invasion of kitchen ants, Kyra sat down to write a poem, something she had not done since applying to medical school. That morning she felt an urgent need to capture all the thoughts racing through her head on paper. When she had finished writing, what she saw on the pages before her was a new vision for her life—a vision that did not include surgery, status, or typical notions of security.

A woman of Native American ancestry, Kyra believed that a vision is to be followed if given. She had not asked for a new life course, and the vision laid out in the poem was different from the path she thought she wanted. Kyra's *moment of obligation* shook her world. Responding to it meant changing her career entirely, a prospect that scared her. She had invested nearly nine years in preparing for medical school and was tens of thousands of dollars in debt. Furthermore, she knew that cancer research was beneficial to others and that there was no reason she should not

Prescription for Change

Dr. **Kyra Bobinet** never imagined that her career would involve helping incarcerated youths. In 1994, she was a first-year student at the University of California, San Francisco (UCSF), School of Medicine, focused single-mindedly on cancer research and a future in surgery. Kyra was certain that this path would satisfy her desire to help others and give her the credentials and recognition that would make her family proud. By the end of her first semester, she had been elected class co-president, joined a prestigious research laboratory as a Dean's research scholar, pursue it. But she was also certain that her life would lose meaning if she did not follow this vision. She felt sure that the poem had revealed her true calling. She had a clear choice: play it safe or surrender to the unknown.

A moment of obligation means following what calls you.

Kyra felt strongly that her new path should involve helping young people, so she accepted an invitation from fellow medical students Huong Huynh and Jennifer Danek to volunteer in UCSF's MedTeach program. In this program, medical students taught classes about health and behavioral issues to young offenders at San Francisco's Youth Guidance Center.

During one of her first classes, Kyra watched as a fellow medical student struggled to control a student's behavior. As the session ended, a violent fight started between two boys. Kyra had seen the fight coming throughout the class. She had felt a "knowing," as if she could see into how the young people's minds and hearts operated, and she wanted to reach out to them.

Being surrounded by young people stimulated and challenged Kyra in a way her medical studies did not. In particular, she was humbled by the young people's total honesty. They did not hide behind social graces like those in professional or academic environments; they called her on her ego, her inconsistency, and her need to be liked. Their survival depended on their ability to read people, and they offered her a mirror in which to see herself.

"The youth were brutally honest about what they saw in me. If I was arrogant, they'd reflect that back to me. If I was competitive, they'd rebel. They'd call me out with their behavior. This was beautiful training for who I wanted to be—it pulled out the best and worst parts of me."

—Kyra Bobinet

While volunteering at the center every week, Kyra struggled with two different emotions: the joy of teaching and working with young people and the sadness of relinquishing her long-held identity as an aspiring surgeon. She cried occasionally as she let her career aspirations go, but she was drawn through compassion toward the young people.

A moment of obligation is bolstered by a deep connection to an issue or a community.

While listening to the incarcerated youths' stories, Kyra and her colleagues realized that there were large gaps in the support systems that should be in place for these young men. Many expressed a desire to build productive, successful lives, but because they received insufficient support, they quickly returned to juvenile hall. Kyra, Jennifer, and members of their community believed the youth would benefit from a more comprehensive approach that would offer them practical life services and self-knowledge training, all from people dedicated to forming long-term, supportive relationships with them. After doing research, Kyra, Jennifer, and a small group of other founders began creating a new organization to better serve these young people.

After Kyra graduated from medical school, she decided to fulfill her *moment of obligation* by pursuing the development of this new organization full-time. In 1998, she and Jennifer secured seed money from Echoing Green and founded Vision Youthz in San Francisco,

California. The organization's mission is to empower young people to gain self-awareness, fulfill their potential, and transform unhealthy behavior. The program is primarily geared toward young men ages fourteen to twenty-one who have been incarcerated, helping them avoid becoming repeat offenders by providing services including self-esteem programs, job placement, and education. Vision Youthz helps the young men understand the relationship between their inner life and their actions.

"When I made the decision to leave medicine, I was more afraid of losing my true path than I was attached to all the security and accolades in the world. Surrendering to this, I have led a far richer and more meaningful life than I ever knew possible."
—Kyra Bobinet

Vision Youthz has had remarkable success. From 2000 to 2005, for example, the organization targeted some of the most chronic, serious juvenile offenders in its community and lowered the recidivism rate in this group to just 25 percent. To put that number in context, a control group not enrolled in Vision Youthz programming post-detention had a recidivism rate of 78 percent, a number similar to the national recidivism average of 80 percent among members of this population. Vision Youthz clients have left gangs, found employment, finished high school, started college, promoted disease prevention through street outreach, attended meditation classes, hiked to the top of Cloud's Rest peak in Yosemite National Park, and much more. Some youth have volunteered as instructors in the detention-based inner-awareness training classes, while others have gone on to join other youth organizations as staff and leaders. Vision Youthz volunteers contribute over 3,000 hours of direct service every year, sending the message that the youth are indispensable members of the community.

Kyra's *moment of obligation* began as a bold new vision. It succeeded because she was not afraid to find out what practical form her vision could take. Her original plan to become a practicing doctor, while set aside, did ultimately lead her to the work that became her passion. Kyra does not believe that a *moment of obligation* has to be dramatic (although hers was!). It can be something more subtle: an adjustment of the lens through which you see the world. Opening yourself up to a *moment of obligation* is not easy. Doing so means acknowledging that your current actions do not reflect your passion. "If you've drifted away from your purpose or at least your impression of it, then what must bring you back is a louder, more intense awakening," Kyra explains.

Fear of the unknown is a powerful reason to maintain the status quo, yet fear can be a signal that you are on to something important. It can mean that the new path is different and uncharted but also worth following. In this context, fear means *go*, not *wait* or *stop*. You must be willing to surrender to fear in order to pursue a *moment of obligation*. And, as Kyra says, continuing along a path you know to be wrong is actually more frightening than taking a new, unknown path.

In a moment of obligation, fear means go.

Kyra's work with Vision Youthz was as much a private journey as a public one. First, she had to change her ideas about how she could best contribute to the world. She also had to leave behind the person she was, reconstituting herself and drawing on reservoirs of strength while growing into her new work. Kyra describes this process as "ego bereavement." She had to mourn the loss of the life and self she knew, including her plans to become a practicing doctor, before she could boldly devote herself to a new path.

> "What brings happiness is facing your fear and being uncomfortable and still finding joy in the midst of everything."
>
> —Kyra Bobinet

Kyra continues to deepen and share her unique learnings on adult-teen relations, an approach to working with young people she calls "teenwhispering." Today, she uses these methods to train adults across the country, helping to transform them into powerful advocates for young people.

Why Is a Moment of Obligation Bold?

A *moment of obligation* is the discovery of your power to make a change—a life-altering, perspective-shifting, courageous change. A *moment of obligation* is preceded by many signs and clues. Recognizing a *moment of obligation* means choosing a pathway and pursuing it, however different it is from the journey you may have envisioned. A *moment of obligation* enables you to **Be Bold** by helping you discover what's most important. Responding to a *moment of obligation* is *your* choice for *your* life. It is a commitment to stand up for your beliefs and to be part of the solution.

Consider This

- How well do you know yourself? Do you pay attention to the internal and external clues that signal your interest in something? What types of stories in the media make you most excited or most upset? What keeps you awake at night? What gets you up in the morning? What global issues are really important to you?

- Why have you gotten involved in certain activities or issues in the past? What has held your interest or prompted you to learn more about a particular issue?

- Can you remember an experience that was really important and meaningful to you that you never followed up on because it seemed too new and different? Have you been afraid to pursue something because it didn't fit with the expectations of yourself and others?

Be Bold

Karen Tse, Echoing Green Fellow, in Geneva, Switzerland

Chapter Two

Gall to Think Big

Taking on the World

The social problems of our time—such as poverty, hunger, homelessness, and educational inequities—are complex and deeply rooted. Many people turn away because these problems are too overwhelming, painful, or removed from their daily lives. Some people, responding to faith, family, or their own *moments of obligation*, choose to get involved and make a difference. Doing charitable work through volunteerism and public service, donating money and resources, or working in the nonprofit sector are key ways to ease the suffering of the less fortunate. On the other hand, working for social change requires you to **Be Bold** and to envision big solutions to big social problems.

Bold thinkers have the gall to challenge the status quo and ask the really hard questions: Why should one citizen matter less than another? What stands in the way of equal opportunity for all? Why shouldn't the wealth of a society be measured by its service and commitment to others? These thinkers have the gall to dismiss the limitations society can place on those with new and different ideas. They transcend the limitations they place on themselves and their dreams because they believe they can take on the world and make a real impact. Quite simply, they have the *gall to think big*.

Those with the *gall to think big* are "practical idealists." Their idealism is boundless and constant—a North Star that carries them through doubt and challenges. Their confidence and ability to self-affirm help them press for the change they wish to see in the world. Yet they do not dismiss reality or insist on an unrelentingly positive view of the world. With hard work and a willingness to learn from their mistakes, these audacious thinkers learn how to execute their visions and bring a high level of strategic thinking to their ideas and organizations. This makes them effective as well as visionary leaders.

Thinking Big on a Global Scale

Karen Tse was born outside of Cleveland, Ohio, to immigrant parents from Hong Kong. She remembers hearing disturbing stories of torture and abuse in Asia whispered among Chinese American neighbors in her community. Karen's childhood was marked by recurring nightmares of political prisoners being beaten as she watched helplessly.

Karen's high-school and college years were shaped by her activism. While in college, she became the president of her campus's Asian Students Association, a powerful group that fostered connections among Asian and Asian American students. Through letter-writing campaigns on behalf of political prisoners and at cross-cultural conferences, she witnessed the power generated by bringing people together across borders to work on common problems.

Being Bold is building a personal vision for positive change.

After earning a law degree from UCLA, Karen worked for three years as a public defender in San Francisco and then landed a job as a human rights lawyer for the United Nations. Her first assignment brought her to postwar Cambodia, which was still traumatized following the four-year rule of the Khmer Rouge, the brutal communist regime responsible for the deaths of an estimated 1.7 million people. When Karen arrived, this country of 13 million citizens was served by only ten remaining lawyers. Working diligently to help build the country's rule of law, she trained judges, prosecutors, and the country's first core group of public defenders; set up Cambodia's first arraignment court; and educated prison guards and police about prisoners' rights. Her work was central in the creation of the Cambodian Defenders Project and Legal Aid of Cambodia,

which are still influential groups in the country.

Everything changed for Karen one day in 1994 when she met a twelve-year-old Cambodian boy who had been imprisoned for stealing a bicycle. The child had been beaten by the police and was confused and terrified about what might happen to him next. There was no set date for his trial. The prison guards were unfazed by their charge's young age, his bruises, and his abandonment by the legal system.

For Karen, in that moment, the boy represented the legions of people around the world who are imprisoned without the basic right to a humane and fair criminal justice system. Ordinary citizens such as that boy do not possess the symbolic power and importance of political prisoners. As a result, they are invisible and voiceless. Karen realized that, as a college student, she never would have written a letter on this child's behalf, as she had done for numerous political prisoners—and that troubled her greatly.

Karen's volunteer experience had shown her the importance of bringing groups together to form a united front. It became clear to her that in order to change the legal system for everyone, the human rights of ordinary criminal defendants would have to be fought for alongside the human rights of political prisoners.

As a United Nations lawyer, Karen and her team had made significant inroads in Cambodia. Yet she knew that Cambodia was only the tip of the iceberg. Burgeoning criminal defense lawyers and public defenders throughout Southeast Asia, particularly in Vietnam and China, needed training and support to help implement their own domestic criminal laws consistent with human rights decrees. At that time, there were few organizations focused on building fair and functioning criminal justice systems around the world.

Starting a new organization to address this need was not something Karen wanted to do. The problem seemed far too daunting for her to take on at the time. She also was being pulled by something else.

The gall to think big starts with a moment of obligation.

Despite Karen's successes in Cambodia, she decided to fulfill a lifelong spiritual calling by enrolling in Harvard's Divinity School—a program she deferred over ten years prior. However, as she fulfilled

her course work to become a Unitarian Universalist minister, she had a nagging feeling that her human rights work was not done. She knew the lack of fair and functioning criminal justice systems around the world continued to adversely affect millions of ordinary citizens. In her final year in divinity school, she wrote a plan for an organization that would expand on her work in Cambodia and use a spiritual framework to confront the problem. For Karen, the work still seemed too overwhelming.

Karen began her life as an ordained minister marrying joyous couples and easing families' sorrow in times of death. All the while, she tracked work on criminal justice system reform globally and was disturbed by the overall lack of progress. Unwilling to ignore her vision for a second time and armed with the support of her spirituality, she was ready to take action and finally respond to her *moment of obligation*.

In 2000, Karen went back to the concept paper she had developed in divinity school and started an organization called International Bridges to Justice (IBJ). IBJ's mission is to address human rights abuses by building and enhancing public defender and other criminal justice structures in developing countries. IBJ argues that prisoners' access to counsel, rights to a fair and timely trial, and freedom from forced confessions are not only basic human rights, but also important indicators of free, open, and democratic societies.

"I've always had very strong feelings for prisoners— they're on the bottom of the totem pole. I believe that our treatment of people worldwide can shift based on our treatment of them."

—Karen Tse

The gall to think big has as much to do with the breadth of your vision as it does with your ability to carry it out. Visionary leaders are simply audacious when confronting obstacles. They go around them. They knock them down. They refuse to be deterred. When Karen launched IBJ's work in China, she had no contacts there and no funding for the organization. She did not speak Mandarin, the language in which business negotiations are conducted, and she could barely afford a translator. But she did not let anything get in her way. She was determined to overcome the many obstacles in her path.

To establish IBJ, Karen moved to Switzerland. By basing itself in Geneva, which is home to many international nongovernmental organizations (NGOs), quasi-governmental agencies, and human rights organizations, IBJ solidified its image as a serious organization. Karen logged hundreds of hours and thousands of miles on airplanes, flying to and within China. She introduced herself to government officials and lawyers, gaining their trust and enlisting them in her cause.

Even before IBJ was big, Karen had the ability to make it *seem* big in order to gain the attention and respect of Chinese governmental bodies and other key groups. People were impressed that the head of the organization attended meetings; Karen jokes that only she knew that the head of the organization was also the only member of the organization. She notes: "What gave IBJ credibility at the beginning was that we seemed big. The executive director was dealing with them directly; the bigwig was coming in. Of course, I was the only wig, the big wig and the small wig." In the beginning, Karen used her own money and donations from friends to get IBJ started. Eventually she connected to funders such as Echoing Green and George Soros's Open Society

Institute, bringing them into her vision as partners.

> "Once I decided to start International Bridges to Justice, I was absolutely obsessed. I thought about it day and night—brushing my teeth, eating my cereal. I couldn't get it out of my mind."
>
> —Karen Tse

IBJ was not an instant success, but the victories eventually came. At the same time that she launched IBJ, Karen negotiated a groundbreaking Memorandum of Understanding (MOU) with the Chinese government to work with them in instituting a criminal legal development program within the Chinese National Legal Aid Center, which is the country's legal services system. Karen's *gall to think big* was not just a symbolic gesture. The MOU made it real.

In 2002 and 2003, IBJ printed more than half a million posters and brochures outlining the rights of Chinese citizens accused of a crime. These materials were distributed by 3,000 law students who were mobilized across the country. IBJ has carried out "advisement of rights" campaigns in virtually every province in China, involving more than half a million Chinese citizens. IBJ also trained over 500 criminal defense lawyers in China, helped support 2,800 legal aid offices, and held over fifty mini-conferences to showcase the best practices and the progress made in China's legal system. Karen has now begun replicating her work in Cambodia and Vietnam and has plans to train leaders to carry on this work across the globe.

Part of Karen's *gall to think big* was her ability to clearly visualize IBJ in full detail before it existed. She compares her vision for IBJ to a glacier: others could see what lay on top but not what floated beneath the surface. She saw the entire magnificent glacier, both above and below the water. It was this clear and expansive vision that fueled Karen and gave her confidence right from IBJ's inception.

The **gall to think big** means seeing what others do not yet see.

Karen credits her success both to her practice of continual self-affirmation and to her ability to take action and persevere in her work. Growing up in the 1960s as a Chinese American girl, first in the Midwest and then in Los Angeles, Karen often struggled against internalizing the stereotypes directed at her by young classmates, neighbors, the media, and even family. She felt loved and adored, but from a young age, she realized that in the eyes of some, her gender decreased her value. Her well-meaning paternal grandmother repeatedly shook her index finger at Karen and said, "Just remember, you are a girl. You only count half." In the end, her grandmother's mantra and stereotyping had the opposite effect: To combat them, she developed a remarkable ability to block out negativity and create a strong self-image.

Self-affirmation, which Karen defines as having an unwavering belief in yourself and finding the courage to act, was pivotal in her *gall to think big* and launch IBJ. When you take on tough issues and dream on a large scale, you cannot depend on others to affirm your goals for you. Many people scoffed at Karen's plans. Her parents found it preposterous that she would imagine taking on the legal system in China, the world's most populous country. Many lawyers, businesspeople, and NGO leaders dismissed her idea for IBJ as, at best,

unrealistic and, at worst, impossible. Even those who believed in the need for an organization like IBJ thought the problems it would tackle were too daunting to address. Karen says, "I think I had at least a hundred people telling me to get a 'real job' and that IBJ wasn't going to work. There was a lot of discouragement in a lot of different places. And yet, if you self-affirm and believe what you believe, you just move forward, in spite of what everyone else says."

"You should take whatever gift you have, find your own genius, celebrate it—and give that gift to the world."
—Karen Tse

Now, years after the launch of IBJ, Karen believes that the journey resulting from the *gall to think big* is what matters most. Even if that journey ends in failure, you will become a different person along the way. Regardless of success or failure, nothing has been wasted, "because you've gained yourself in being true to yourself." Today, Karen continues to turn inward for inspiration. She shares her spiritual strength with the staff of IBJ, gathering with them each day at the office for a period of reflection followed by the reading of a text with an insightful message. This spiritual focus sustains her and her team, especially when they are faced with shortages of funds, criticism, and other setbacks.

The gall to think big requires inner reserves of strength.

Ultimately, the *gall to think big* means knowing that you are part of something larger than yourself or your particular effort. The task of securing justice for prisoners around the world extends beyond IBJ's work, and the knowledge that she is part of a bigger cause inspires Karen. She sees IBJ not as a legal program, but as part of a people's movement—a movement that can engage everyone, from a farmer to a policeman. IBJ already depends on courageous individuals who put themselves and their lives on the line and speak out about their rights. Karen believes countless others will also fight for human rights if shown an effective way to do so. One of Karen's long-term goals is to give all people, not just lawyers and activists, the opportunity to contribute by creating thousands of "communities of conscience." This would allow the general population to support emerging legal aid centers worldwide.

The gall to think big involves recognizing your essential, yet humble, role in a larger movement.

Due to the success of their work in Asia, IBJ's offices have received a flood of inquiries from all over world, from lawyers and citizens experiencing the same legal challenges. They have asked IBJ for help in implementing newly established criminal laws in their countries. With the *gall to think big* never far away, Karen is currently developing an international defender institute to support the work of legal defenders through a worldwide fellowship program. As inspiration, Karen cites advice from a Buddhist monk under whom she studied meditation in Cambodia: *Whatever you focus on will grow.* In order to act on their *gall to think big*, leaders like Karen apply attention and concrete action to their original grand visions.

"I believe this work is possible. The question is whether we, as a global community, have a commitment to making it happen."

—Karen Tse

freshman-year roommate, a gifted poet, struggle with her coursework. Wendy's roommate told her about attending public high school in challenging circumstances in the South Bronx, New York. Wendy was troubled by the inequality between her educational experience and her roommate's; she knew that her high-school education gave her a significant advantage at Princeton.

Being Bold is setting goals as realistic as they are ambitious.

A Movement Begins With an Idea

Wendy Kopp grew up in a comfortable neighborhood in Dallas, Texas. The public high school she attended, which was comparable to a top private school, spent ample resources on infrastructure, athletics, and other extracurricular activities. It was assumed that Wendy, like most of her classmates, would graduate and attend college. In the fall of 1984, Wendy matriculated at Princeton University.

Wendy's interest in educational policy was sparked during her first weeks at Princeton as she watched her

As a public policy major, Wendy studied this country's educational system. After deciding to make real what she was only reading about in books, she organized a conference that connected students with business leaders to discuss the nation's education problems. Rising student enrollment and an impending surge in teacher retirement meant that the United States was headed toward a decade of teacher shortages. Poor rural areas and big cities were already feeling these shortages, and student performance was suffering as a result. In urban and rural areas, an elementary-school child worked at a level three grades behind his or her counterpart in wealthier suburbs. And a child born into urban communities, such as the Bronx or Compton, was seven times less likely to graduate from college than a child born in Manhattan or Beverly Hills. During one session at the conference, many students expressed interest in teaching at public schools as a way of combating these educational inequities.

With the conference over and graduation looming, Wendy began looking for a job. But nothing struck her as the right fit. Many of her friends were also struggling to find the right careers. Investment banks and consulting firms recruited aggressively on campus. Some students accepted two-year positions at these companies in the hopes that they would learn a lot and then pursue more public-service-oriented careers. Other graduating seniors, including Wendy, looked for a direct pathway to service immediately after graduation.

Wendy was required to write a senior thesis in order to graduate. Sensing an opportunity, she began pulling together the many threads of her personal and educational experiences. She decided that bright college graduates who were searching for meaningful, challenging careers might find fulfillment by working in underserved schools. Wendy envisioned an initiative in which new college graduates would be recruited for teaching jobs just as they were recruited for positions in investment banking

and consulting. The talent and energy of these new graduates could be the perfect solution to an enduring problem. As teachers, recent graduates could have an immense impact on the lives of disadvantaged children. In turn, the teaching experience would help shape the recruits' lifelong career paths and affirm their civic commitment.

"I understood the mind-set of college seniors because I was one."

—Wendy Kopp

Wendy's thesis became the blueprint for her new idea, which she called Teach For America. Wendy's detailed business plan relied on her *gall to think big*. She proposed a first-year budget of $2.5 million and an initial corps of 500 teachers, talented recent college graduates who would commit to teaching two years in both urban and rural underserved schools across the United States. Wendy's research underscored the enormity of education problems in the United States, and she was certain that effecting any sort of systemic change would require starting big. She believed that reforming education to eliminate inequities had to be a sweeping *movement*, not a gesture, and she envisioned Teach For America as an important part of that movement. Her goals were audacious, but Wendy firmly believed they were attainable.

"I wouldn't say that every organization should start with 500 members. Every idea has its own natural starting point. In our case, I believe that starting at this scale was critical as a way to convey the importance and urgency of the effort."

—Wendy Kopp

Wendy's trajectory reminds us that the *gall to think big* is as much about a deep base of knowledge as it is about vision. In order to address a problem fully, you need to learn every aspect of it, including its history, trends, key statistics, supporting data, current and proposed policy measures, the economics of the problem, and the major players in the field. Once you have gained comprehensive knowledge of a problem, you can develop a vision that is grounded in practical strategies.

Wendy's approach to learning was an academic one: she used her college career to study educational inequities in the U.S. Through writing her senior thesis and shoring up the knowledge she had already gained from classes, her conference, and discussions with classmates, she was able to envision a solution to a problem close to her heart. But Wendy's approach is not the only one possible. Practical and experiential learning can be just as useful.

The **gall to think big** means learning all you can about a problem in order to identify the smartest solution.

Wendy moved to turn her senior thesis into a funding proposal. She tracked down the addresses of some thirty CEOs and business leaders and requested meetings to ask for support. Wendy had never met any of the people she was approaching. She was not a recognized education expert. She had not yet graduated from college. All she had was a remarkable entrepreneurial spirit, coupled with a willingness to do whatever was necessary to make her idea become a reality.

The **gall to think big** means pursuing your own pathway despite skepticism from others or seemingly insurmountable challenges.

43

While her classmates celebrated their imminent graduation, Wendy put on a business suit and, proposal in hand, started taking the early train into New York City from Princeton to ask for money. Her thesis adviser asked if she understood how difficult it was to raise $25,000, let alone the $2.5 million Wendy had proposed as an initial budget. But by the end of the summer after graduation, Wendy had been given office space from Morgan Stanley in Manhattan, established a founding board, and received corporate support from the Mobil Corporation and a seed grant from Echoing Green.

Wendy aggressively set about recruiting, selecting, training, and placing in schools the 500 teachers who would make up the first corps of Teach For America. This large-scale beginning gave Teach For America momentum and a sense of national importance that Wendy believed was critical to attracting the most sought-after graduates. "Teach For America quickly attracted hundreds of people, who were drawn both to the core belief and idea of the importance of educational equity as well as the power and simplicity of the Teach For America mission," Wendy says.

A social movement—a collective action in which individuals, groups, and organizations unite to carry out social change—is often sparked when a large number of people realize that others share their values and desire for a particular change. One of the many challenges facing an emerging social movement is exactly how to spread the news that it exists. Teach For America created a visible outlet, enabling disparate groups that cared about the same thing to come together. Even though the business leaders who supported Wendy doubted that Teach For America could attract enough young applicants, they understood the crisis in our nation's public schools and felt compelled to act. The young people whom Wendy contacted had no expertise in the field of education, but as Wendy knew, they were looking for something meaningful to do with their lives.

Charismatic leadership, such as Wendy's rallies, forces and provides a voice calling for change. Although the leadership of one person is an important part of movement building, it is only one component. Social movements are grounded in time and place and are catalyzed when the right forces come together—forces beyond any one individual's control. Wendy says, "If I hadn't thought of this idea, I have no doubt that someone else would have."

> **The gall to think big means understanding the mechanics of movement building.**

Today, Teach For America fields over 4,000 teachers annually, who work in over 1,000 schools in twenty-two regions, with a goal to reach an 8,000-member corps by 2010. It took ten years to build a stable organization with 1,000 corps members per year, and another six to reach the 4,000 mark. Movement building and social change are long-term propositions. Wendy is in it for the long haul and continues to do the math.

entered the consciousness of the younger generation. In 2006, Teach For America received almost 19,000 applications for its teaching program, including applications from 10 percent of the graduating classes of schools such as Spelman, Yale, and Dartmouth.

> "I never consciously thought I was thinking big for the sake of it. I just thought this idea had to happen."
> —Wendy Kopp

> "I always thought Teach For America would be where it is today, with a corps of several thousand teachers—I just thought we'd get here much sooner."
> —Wendy Kopp

Today, more than 12,000 Teach For America alumni work across the country, filling leadership positions in the fields of education, business, and policy. This small army of education reform activists fights locally, regionally, and nationally for educational equity. Furthermore, Teach For America has

As Wendy marks her second decade at the helm of Teach For America, she is no longer a college wunderkind, and her organization is no longer a daring upstart. Teach For America is a mature, nationally recognized nonprofit organization with a $55 million annual budget and over 350 staff members. It is one of only twenty-one direct-service, nonprofit organizations (excluding hospitals, museums, universities, etc.) founded since 1971 to have a budget over $20 million. Wendy is projecting an annual budget for Teach For America of $100 million in the next five years. She is a seasoned nonprofit professional who has received much praise and many awards in recognition of her accomplishments, including the Citizen Activist Award from the Gleitsman Foundation, the John F. Kennedy New Frontier Award, Aetna's Voice of Conscience Award, and the Jefferson Award for Public Service. In addition to receiving six honorary doctorates, Wendy was the youngest person and the first woman to receive Princeton's Woodrow Wilson Award, the highest honor the school confers on its undergraduate alumni.

What hasn't changed is Wendy's idealism, her laserlike focus on Teach For America's mission, and her inner strength—all qualities that gave her the *gall to think big* while she was still a college student. She has worked hard to foster a similar set of core organizational values for Teach For America, balancing reaching for the stars with delivering on what is promised. "A goal should be ambitious—but it has to be feasible," Wendy says. You must find the intersection between "stretch" and realism and operate there. Without lofty goals, you have nothing to work toward; without realistic goals, you have no hope of success. Teach For America talks about these core values in terms of "thinking openly with a sense of possibility" and "disciplined thought."

> "'Disciplined thought' means to reflect constantly on what we learn from experience, inform our decisions with data, and make decisions that are deeply rooted in our mission. This practice is part of the fabric of our organization."
> —Wendy Kopp

In the story of Teach For America's first decade, *One Day, All Children ... The Unlikely Triumph of Teach For America and What I Learned Along the Way*, Wendy provides a valuable "how-to" and "how-not-to" manual for aspiring nonprofit leaders. As the title of her book suggests, Wendy is anything but smug or self-satisfied, and she openly discusses the many mistakes that resulted in budgetary cash-flow problems, public-relations firestorms, and low staff and corps morale. One entire section of her book is appropriately called "The Dark Years." But it was through that bumpy process that she learned the importance of building solid organizational systems and instilling core values. Wendy's story reveals the power of the *gall to think big*. You press on because you must and because your idea for change truly matters.

The Power of Idealism

Shirley Chisholm, the first African American woman elected to Congress, once said: "Service is the rent you pay for room on this earth." Public service enriches individuals, helping them to develop competence as well as compassion. It teaches civic responsibility and strengthens communities. And it helps those in need.

Being Bold is the synergy between passion and action.

Michael Brown *gets* service. He grew up in a family that discussed justice,

ethics, and "giving back" around the dinner table. He watched his parents participate in countless volunteer activities in their community, and he was an active volunteer himself during his teenage years. He took a year off between his sophomore and junior years of college to work on Capitol Hill, assisting a congressman on legislation proposing a voluntary national service program. After graduating from college, Michael spent a year working with a community service program in New York City.

The gall to think big means continually changing the way you view a problem.

Michael went to Harvard Law School in 1985. He spent three years studying law and broadening his thinking about an array of topics, including justice, citizenship, and equality. Like most graduate students, he spent a lot of time studying and a lot of nights eating takeout and debating the state of the world. Michael and his law-school roommate and lifelong friend, Alan Khazei, engaged in conversations of consequence that would change their lives forever. They spent countless hours discussing the social problems in the United States and wondering how so much disparity could exist in

47

a country so wealthy. But they also marveled at the economic boom that was under way in the 1980s, fueled by brash entrepreneurs whose innovative thinking created astonishing levels of new wealth and smashed old norms and business methods. They were disturbed by the community disengagement and racial polarization that they witnessed and read about. But they also were optimistic about the power of one individual to make a difference and the power of the ideal that is America and all it stands for.

> "Once you find your passion, it's easy to think big. Your passion fuels you."
> —Michael Brown

Using their dorm room as a think tank, Michael and Alan unleashed the *gall to think big*, imagining a national community full of idealism and dedicated to service. They believed that if a democratic society is to work and thrive, its citizens must participate in significant ways. As Michael and Alan knew, they were members of only the thirteenth generation of United States citizens since the American Revolution. They felt there was something

fundamentally lacking in the American experience; it was too easy for each person to lead an entirely private life with no real sense of civic responsibility. Michael thought that at the heart of this problem lay the tension between two competing views of America: as a beacon of democracy and justice on the one hand, and as a land of rugged individualism and self-interest on the other. He worried that many Americans were not aware of current problems and that even those Americans who were and who wanted to do something about them did not know how to take action. Michael and Alan wanted to do no less than strengthen America's democracy through citizen service.

They sensed that people had lost the belief that they could make a difference. Because problems such as homelessness, poverty, and drug abuse seemed so overwhelming, people asked, "What can one person really achieve?" rather than, "What can I do?" Michael and Alan believed public service to be a powerful method of demonstrating to people that they can indeed make a difference, whether by building a playground, repainting a school's peeling walls, or rehabilitating housing for the homeless.

Michael and Alan envisioned young people from all backgrounds coming together in service, forming a group that would be a useful resource in addressing our nation's most pressing societal ills. They studied the United States military system as a model for how young people of all races and from all classes can join together to serve and work. With their *gall to think big*, Michael and Alan envisioned the day when the most commonly asked question of an eighteen-year-old would be, "Where will you do your service year?" Michael and Alan proposed nothing less than a new national call to service that would reinvigorate what it meant to be an American citizen.

Moments of obligation do not wait for convenient times or circumstances. With graduation approaching and students in hot pursuit of offers from law firms, Michael and Alan committed to translating their lofty ideas into action. They began developing an organization that would promote voluntary national service and provide scores of young people with the opportunity to improve their country. They named the organization City Year to reflect its goal of bringing together young people from ethnically and economically diverse backgrounds for a year of service.

Neither a youth job-training program nor a service-learning project, City Year was to be something entirely different, something bigger. It aimed to change the way young people came of age in this country, making service a universal experience.

The gall to think big involves planning for long-term change.

Michael and Alan eventually planned to create a national yearlong program, but before rolling out the program fully, they wanted to test their idea, identify and manage early mistakes, and refine the concept. In 1988, City Year recruited a diverse group of young people and conducted an eight-week summer pilot program. Participants in the program volunteered throughout the Boston area with organizations that worked with the elderly and the disabled, ran affordable housing programs, and protected the environment.

Emboldened by the success of the pilot program, Michael and Alan geared up to start the first yearlong program in Boston. They received start-up grants from a few groups, including Echoing Green, and began hiring staff, fundraising, spreading the word among young people, and working tirelessly to spark interest in the organization.

49

In 1989, the first group of fifty City Year corps members fanned out across Boston, completing more than twenty-five community service projects during their service year.

Launching a new organization or any new project can be overwhelming, exhausting, and scary. But there was nothing Michael wanted to do more. He took to heart the famous words of Joseph Campbell, author, professor, and intellectual: "Follow your bliss."

The gall to think big means being very clear about why your actions will deliver results.

Each idea for social transformation is grounded in a theory of change—a set of predictions about how change will happen as a result of a certain program. A well-thought-out theory considers the conditions necessary for change to occur, defines success, plans for how success can be achieved, and identifies short-, medium-, and long-term goals. Even though Michael and Alan were just starting City Year, they had thought a great deal about its theory of change.

Michael's faith in the American people made him confident that City Year would succeed. He believed that Americans would want to make their communities better and leave their mark on the world. Michael was able to generate a collective vision rather than one based on the leadership of one great person. He knew that people could be instructed on how to organize groups, find resources, and develop and execute logical plans. But he also believed that with the right tools and instruction, an individual could learn how to expand the scope of his or her imagination. He believed that idealism could actually be taught as one component of a set of skills that included the ability to solve problems, visualize alternatives, and take practical steps to create change. For Michael and Alan, strengthening our democracy through citizen service became their equation for change.

"If you put good out into the world, good will come back to you. You're creating pathways for people to unite."
—Michael Brown

City Year has grown exponentially since that first pilot program in Boston in the summer of 1988. The program now fields over 1,200 youth service corps members each year in sixteen cities and fourteen states. It has even started its first corps outside of the United States in South Africa. Since its inception, City Year has engaged more than 915,000 citizens in service, provided more than 13 million hours of service, and worked with more than 900,000 children around the U.S. The organization now has an annual budget of more than $44 million.

With the *gall to think big* comes the willingness to pull any and all levers of change to fulfill your vision. For Michael and Alan, engaging in public policy-making is a critical and effective strategy for achieving their ultimate goal of a voluntary national service system. Public policy can be defined as the sum of government activities. Public policies greatly impact our public and private lives, set the country's agenda, and influence the flow of resources nationwide. Involvement in the process allows individuals, groups, organizations, and coalitions to have an important voice.

In 1991, after President George H. W. Bush established the Commission on National and Community Service, City Year received its first federal funding: a grant from the Commission. That same year, Michael and Alan invited all of the presidential candidates, including then-governor Bill Clinton, to add a visit to City Year headquarters to their campaign schedules. Bill Clinton's visit strengthened his resolve to implement AmeriCorps, his vision of a nationwide, federally funded service initiative that he saw demonstrated in City Year's model.

"If you're involved in the social sector, you need to stay involved in the larger social change objective. You need to leverage your work from a policy perspective."
—Michael Brown

Since President Clinton created AmeriCorps in 1994, more than 400,000 citizens have served their nation by working with more than 2,500 nonprofit and faith-based organizations. In 2003, when AmeriCorps suffered huge budget cuts, City Year helped organize the Save AmeriCorps Coalition to promote the value of and encourage support for national service. This same coalition worked successfully to get a record $444 million appropriation from Congress for AmeriCorps for 2005. Each budget cycle, the coalition continues the challenging work of insuring that adequate funding is maintained and promoting the growth of AmeriCorps.

The gall to think big means understanding that the consequences of your actions last well beyond your lifetime.

City Year is Michael's life's work. It is the ultimate expression of his beliefs and values, his own idealism and commitment, and his unwavering faith in the power of young people to make a positive impact on the world. He believes in the inherent idealism of young people and their potential to act in positive ways when confronted with unjust situations.

Young people have inherited this world and all the injustices in it. They understand that others wait behind them, inheriting their legacy and benefiting or suffering from the consequences of their actions. Michael believes that as the Iroquois proverb says, you should consider the effects of your actions on the next *seven* generations. What you do matters now and will continue to matter, for better or for worse, long after you are gone. There is a lot at stake. Michael says, "I advise young people not to just own the received paths of their life, but to take calculated risks for the civic good. It's part of the civic contract—we all drink from the wells that other people dig. There is something about giving back,

no matter your background. It's more than just participating in society. It's the possibility that you may find your bliss."

Have the Gall to Think Big

The *gall to think big* means not just being involved in an issue you care about but taking it on so completely that you help catalyze large-scale societal change. It also is about taking bold steps to make something powerful happen, as Karen Tse, Wendy Kopp, and Michael Brown and Alan Khazei have done.

From these three stories, you can draw lessons that will help you take on big challenges: know that big problems require big solutions; have confidence in your vision and let your convictions drive your work forward; learn everything you can about the issues that matter to you in order to come up with new and effective solutions; find the courage to pursue your passion despite obstacles and naysayers; and remember that the results matter just as much as the vision does.

Consider This

- If you had the power to solve one social problem in the world, which one would you choose? How would you go about solving this problem, and what would the world look like once your solution was implemented?

- If you already are working in the nonprofit sector, do you believe fully in the mission and vision of the organization for which you are working? If you have any doubts, what are they? Can you outline your organization's goals clearly? Are they as ambitious as they are realistic?

- Have there been times when you have continued on in the face of doubt or opposition? If so, what kept you going? Do you consider yourself resilient?

- What big ideas do you have that you've never shared with anyone? What's stopping you from sharing them and putting them into action?

Be Bold

Eric Rosenthal, Echoing Green Fellow, in Washington, D.C.

Chapter Three

New and Untested

Your Unique Contribution

Being Bold is about leaving your mark on the world. Innovation is one of the most effective ways to make a real difference. By creating *new* ideas, services, and practices, innovation improves the way things are done in a particular field. Innovation can stem from completely new ideas or from existing ideas connected in new and effective ways.

Do not underestimate the courage it takes to innovate and propose something *new and untested*. When you point out the ineffectiveness of current strategies, you may be seen as a threat to the status quo and to commonly held beliefs. Putting a *new and untested* idea into practice may require you to work outside the mainstream, at least at first. You may be ignored or even attacked. You must be entrepreneurial in order to gather the resources needed to test your new idea. And you will have to rely on something larger than yourself—your family, friends, and mentors; your beliefs and values; your spiritual grounding—to guide you through uncharted territory.

Embracing the *new and untested* allows you to dream in a socially useful way and then make it a reality.

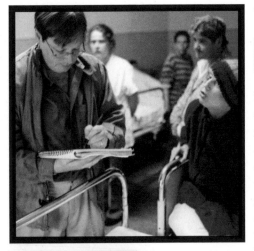

Making the Connection

Eric Rosenthal was one day away from leaving Mexico. A young attorney fresh out of law school, he was there in 1992 working with the indigenous people of Chiapas, a severely impoverished group subjected to human rights abuses by the Mexican authorities. On his last night, Eric R.

had dinner with a colleague, another American lawyer working in Mexico. They chatted about their career paths. Eric R. told her that he never intended to be a human rights lawyer—he had actually started his career in the mental health field because he was passionate about protecting the rights of people with mental disabilities.

Being Bold means connecting unrelated ideas in entirely new ways.

New and untested ideas often grow out of our experiences. Eric R.'s journey began in college, where he studied psychology and took premed courses, intending one day to become a psychiatrist. After volunteering at a psychiatric hospital in Chicago, however, he became disillusioned by the field. The extreme marginalization of the patients troubled him. "What I saw in the hospital was dehumanizing. But I didn't have the vocabulary or framework back then to articulate it as a civil rights or human rights abuse."

After graduation, Eric R. went to Israel to help the Israeli peace movement, which exposed him to human rights work in the Palestinian territories. Inspired by Israeli and Palestinian human rights lawyers, he returned to the United States to apply to law school. Poor

LSAT scores forced him to put off law school for a few years. Meanwhile, he took a job as a paralegal at an advocacy organization working to advance the civil rights of people with mental disabilities in the United States.

"The best thing that ever happened to me was that I got horrible LSAT scores."

—Eric Rosenthal

After two years helping people whose rights were abused in the U.S. mental health system, Eric R. finally made it into law school. As a student at Georgetown University's Law School, he wrote a law review article exploring the relationship between mental disability rights and international human rights— and discovered that he had stumbled into a completely new space. No one was doing or even talking about this kind of work, despite the number of important, overlooked protections under international law that were applicable to mental disabilities advocacy.

Having lived and worked in various places around the world, Eric R. was deeply disturbed by the treatment of people with mental disabilities outside of the United States and frustrated by the lack of advocacy efforts on their behalf. He believed that conditions for the mentally disabled worldwide were not just a social issue, but also a human rights issue. After his law review article was published, he reached out to a few organizations, but large human rights groups such as Amnesty International told him that the issue was "outside their mandate," and U.S.-based mental health advocacy groups hesitated to involve themselves in international affairs.

That night at dinner in Mexico, Eric R.'s American colleague said that he should meet a brash Mexican activist who had brought extensive local press attention to the poor conditions in Mexico City's psychiatric facilities.

Envisioning something new and untested means harnessing your skills and experiences while being open to the unfamiliar.

On his way to the airport the next morning, Eric R. and the activist paid a visit to Ramirez Moreno, a sprawling psychiatric institution on the outskirts of Mexico City. Its security ward looked more like a prison than a medical facility, with a barbed-wire fence surrounding it. They walked right through the front door, which was unlocked. "If people don't know they're abusing human rights, they have nothing to hide," Eric R. says.

Getting to the new and untested means questioning the status quo.

In Ramirez Moreno, Eric R. witnessed human rights abuses more horrifying than anything he had ever seen before. The patients lived in total squalor. Most wore shabby clothing or nothing at all. Human excrement and urine covered the floors, walls, and bedsheets. Parts of the campus lacked running water. The patients were so heavily medicated that they could barely walk; many spent their days sprawled naked on a concrete patio.

The institution offered virtually no rehabilitation or treatment. With nothing to do and no one to care for them, many patients resorted to hitting themselves and continuously rocking back and forth. "This behavior is aggravated by long-term institutionalization," says Eric R., "because all people crave some form of stimulus or feeling."

The residents of Ramirez Moreno, some of the most vulnerable citizens of Mexico, had been abandoned by the community, stripped of dignity, and denied access to appropriate medical treatment. Even more heartbreaking was the fact that with treatment and support, many of these residents would have been perfectly capable of living in mainstream society. Eric R. viewed the situation as inhumane. He could not turn away.

"When I went to the Mexican psychiatric institution, I was horrified by what I saw. From that moment, I knew this was what I had to do."
—Eric Rosenthal

The visit to the psychiatric institution marked Eric R.'s *moment of obligation.* Seeing the problems firsthand made him realize that he needed to act boldly and tackle the issue himself. "After that visit in Mexico, I knew I had to set up my own organization. When you see such utter human suffering, when you see people who are being overlooked, you truly see why innovation is needed," Eric R. says.

Eric R.'s American colleague suggested that he apply for an Echoing Green Fellowship to fund the work that existing organizations refused to do.

So Eric R. returned home and created a proposal to start a new organization called Mental Disability Rights International (MDRI), which would promote the human rights of people with mental disabilities, lobby for their integration into society, train a new generation of grassroots activists committed to this issue, document human rights violations in psychiatric institutions around the world, and shame countries into ending these abuses.

Embracing the new and untested means both taking ownership of a problem as well as its innovative solution.

Eric R.'s innovation was to apply international human rights standards to the treatment of people with mental disabilities. At the time MDRI opened, in 1993, no global organization carried out this kind of work. To be taken seriously in the human rights field, Eric R. had to show that the treatment of patients in psychiatric institutions around the world could be categorized as inhumane and degrading, or even as torture. This categorization would put the treatment in conflict with the United Nations human rights conventions.

"Separately, disability rights and international human rights are not new. Making the link is."

—Eric Rosenthal

MDRI started as a *new and untested* idea, but it has become a formidable player on the international human rights scene. Eric R. and his staff have investigated abuses in psychiatric institutions in over twenty countries throughout Latin America, Eastern Europe, and the Middle East. MDRI staff regularly advise organizations such as the United Nations, the World Health Organization, and the Inter-American Commission on Human Rights. After almost fifteen years in the field, MDRI is increasingly seeing members of the mentally disabled community included in discussions on their rights in countries around the world.

Discovering something new and untested requires you to make associations between seemingly disconnected ideas.

In every country MDRI has targeted for action, its work has led to progress. In Hungary, MDRI's work led to new disability rights legislation that protects people in psychiatric institutions. MDRI helped Hungarian activists develop an innovative program where former psychiatric patients work as human rights ombudsmen to monitor the conditions in which their hospitalized peers are living. Progress has not always been easy. For example, it took MDRI many years of advocacy with its international partners to successfully ban the practice of locking mentally disabled patients in cages.

> "When I started my work, people locked up in one of these custodial facilities in Mexico or Argentina rarely ever got to leave the facility and take control of their lives."
>
> —Eric Rosenthal

After MDRI documented patient abuses in numerous Mexican psychiatric facilities, the government agreed to shut down the worst offender and create safe, alternative community-based programs. The Mexican government also hired the chief of psychiatry from San Francisco General Hospital, who had co-authored the MDRI report, to design the new system of government-funded, community-based mental health programs. "The closure of the Mexican facility was one of the most rewarding moments in my professional career," says Eric R.

MDRI has worked most recently in Turkey, taking advantage of the country's bid to join the European Union to press for changes. MDRI's 2005 report exposed the practice of "unmodified ECT," electroshock administered without anesthesia or muscle relaxants, on both adult and child patients in numerous Turkish psychiatric institutions. The World Health Organization has called for a ban on the procedure and stated that children should never be subjected to the treatment. Identifying unmodified ECT as nothing less than torture, MDRI's report received overwhelming press attention in Turkey and Europe and became the subject of a major article and editorial in *The New York Times*. As a result, members of the European Parliament have pledged to hold the government of Turkey accountable for these abuses as the country applies for inclusion into the European Union.

MDRI demonstrates the power of the *new and untested*. In the social sector, new ideas are often what lead to progress in solving tough problems. As Eric R. says, "If there weren't innovation, there would be nothing. This holds even truer for people who have been historically overlooked or excluded by society."

Eric R.'s openness to the *new and untested* stems, in part, from his upbringing. The son of U.S. foreign assistance workers, Eric R. grew up in West Africa and America, an experience he credits with giving him an "outsider's perspective" on both places. The ability to stand apart from something can be liberating; it can also give you the freedom to question, test, and provoke the status quo. Challenging conventions requires enough self-confidence and creativity to move beyond what you know. This unknown territory is where innovation happens.

Discovering something *new and untested* begins when you allow yourself to break down mental barriers and make associations between seemingly disconnected ideas. Eric R.'s extensive traveling, educational opportunities, various jobs, and side interests all helped him to make connections between unlikely concepts— connections that became the foundation for new, exciting ideas. Eric R.'s passion for making a difference turned him into a prolific idea generator. He discarded many ideas, tested others, kept some in the back of his mind, and learned from those that failed.

Not everyone will develop a truly innovative idea for social change, but everyone can be open to the process of innovation, and everyone can approach social issues in new ways. Don't assume that you must accept the current situation or that the way things are right now cannot or should not change. Question the status quo. Question your own beliefs about an issue. Strengthen your creative muscles by learning everything you can about an issue and constantly asking, "Why are things done that way? What if I tried another way?" Most of all, find the courage to create a new path for change. It will be the best risk you ever take.

"When you make a breakthrough with a *new and untested* idea, it is deeply gratifying. You create your own map to achieve your vision."

—Eric Rosenthal

Partners in Innovation

After graduating from a small liberal arts college with degrees in engineering and economics, Eric Adler landed his first teaching job at the prestigious St. Paul's School in Baltimore, Maryland, a private school that charged a five-figure yearly tuition. One of Eric A.'s students, Ethan, came from a low-income, high-crime neighborhood in inner-city Baltimore. Ethan had transferred to St. Paul's from a public school in Baltimore City after receiving a full merit scholarship. He showed great academic aptitude and promise, but he was struggling in his new environment.

Ethan came to school every day weighed down by more than his books. His mother, a single parent, received little support, and her alcohol abuse created a chaotic home life for Ethan and his siblings. He commuted three hours every day, leaving his familiar African American community for a culture as foreign to him as another country.

Being Bold is working together for a common cause.

As Eric A. thought about the challenges facing Ethan, he began to understand the importance of *place* in a child's life. A child's out-of-school environment is just as critical to his or her educational success as is his or her in-school environment. A school like St. Paul's would have to be fundamentally restructured if students like Ethan were to succeed. As a new teacher, Eric A. could not make this restructuring happen. However, he worked closely with Ethan over the course of his high-school career and watched this exceptional young man adapt, succeed, and continue on to a top New England college. Eric. A. believed that there must be a better way to make high-quality college preparatory education more widely available to low-income children of all academic levels.

> **Discovering the new and untested means imagining how the world might be different.**

Eric A.'s passion for education was rooted in his own experience. As a child, he attended a large public school in Montgomery County, Maryland. When he reached high-school age, his parents sent him to Sidwell Friends, a nationally recognized private school in Washington, D.C. It did not take long for Eric A. to realize that he was being given a tremendous opportunity. No matter how good the public school system in Montgomery County, it could not compete with the small class sizes and excellent support systems at private schools like Sidwell Friends. His own public school experience had been a positive one; he imagined how much larger the quality gap between public and private education was for students in distressed and failing public schools.

"Early in high school, I became convinced that the solution to virtually every problem in the world, whether it's drug abuse, poverty, hunger, or homelessness, is education."

—Eric Adler

In the eight years Eric A. spent at St. Paul's as a teacher and administrator, he never stopped learning about the field of education, observing how his prep school worked, and analyzing his own experiences. He continued to be consumed by the challenge of providing high-quality college preparatory education to as many low-income and disadvantaged students as possible. Eric A. knew that exclusive preparatory schools were not the answer for the vast majority of low-income students, who had access only to the public school system, yet he admired the rigor and high expectations of institutions like St. Paul's and Sidwell Friends. Most public schools are neighborhood based, which benefits children by keeping them close to their families, community leaders, and culture. But they may suffer when their schools are in neighborhoods scarred by crime, drugs, poverty, and despair. For Eric A., the question was how to create a first-rate public school education in a safe, structured, success-driven environment. Eric A. had the answer: an urban public boarding school.

> **A new and untested idea is your own novel plan for achieving significant positive change.**

Sometimes, though, the *new* happens on a different schedule than the *testing*. Eric A. enrolled in Wharton business school, planning to become an entrepreneur. After graduation, he surprised himself and his family by accepting a position as a management consultant. After less than a year, however, he realized that while consulting brought in a comfortable six-figure salary, it would not fulfill him for the rest of his life. He started thinking about what his life's work should be and kept returning to his idea for an urban public boarding school. Eric A.'s short stint at the consulting firm turned out to be incredibly valuable, as it helped him sharpen his critical thinking skills and gave him a window into what it takes to run something. He defines an entrepreneur, whether in the business or social sector, as someone who becomes the owner of an idea. Now that he owned this idea of starting an urban public boarding school, it was his responsibility to try to make it a reality.

Eric A. began by talking extensively about his idea. His friends poked holes in the concept, questioned his strategy, and forced him to defend and refine the idea. Talking to people helped Eric A. strengthen his plan as well as build a community of like-minded supporters. This network eventually led him to Rajiv ("Raj") Vinnakota, another management consultant at a competitor firm who also had been talking about the idea of an urban public boarding school.

Eric A. and Raj's *moment of obligation* arrived at the end of an intense weekend gathering of people excited by the prospect of a new urban boarding school in Washington, D.C. After all the brainstorming, theorizing, and planning, the only step remaining was the decision to start the school. Both men remember the pivotal moment in detail: "My wife had baked cookies," Eric A. says. "We were discussing our belief that it would take one or two people full-time to get this school started and we were the only two people left in the room. It was very clear who those two people should be. Raj said, 'You in?' and I said, 'Yeah. I'm in. I wouldn't have come this far if I wasn't.'"

They both quit their jobs the next day.

"It's always nice to find someone to jump off a cliff with you. But we'd both given this idea a decent amount of thought, and both of us decided the time was right to go forward."
—Eric Adler

New and untested ideas can be remarkably fragile. For you and your idea to survive the scrutiny and skepticism that accompany all change, you must have a supportive network. You may find your network by partnering with a like-minded innovator, creating a team of advisers, relying on the wisdom of your mentors, or reaching out to caring family and friends. Eric A. and Raj have a close partnership that is fueled by open and constant communication. "One of the most interesting things about our relationship is how we argue," Eric A. says. "What I sensed in Raj is an intellectual partner who wanted to have the same real arguments as I did, to get at the best answer." Their partnership provides a safe space for creativity, innovation, and risk taking—all in service of low-income children and their access to high-quality education.

"You have to be able to check your ego at the door and say this is about getting to the best decision. It's not about whether Raj or Eric got the best answer."

—Raj Vinnakota

Eric A. and Raj had the *gall to think big.* Their primary innovation lay in bringing a proven model for college preparatory education—the boarding school—to the public education system for low-income kids in urban areas. They envisioned high-performing public boarding schools in inner-city neighborhoods all across the country—schools that would prepare low-income students in grades seven through twelve for college and beyond. In 1997, with Echoing Green as an early investor, they founded The SEED Foundation to execute their vision.

Pursuing the new and untested is understanding that you don't know everything and trusting that you will learn.

Coming up with a new idea is only part of the story. Innovation is as much about planning, following through, and hashing out details as it is about generating ideas. Securing funding was a crucial hurdle for Eric A. and Raj. The year before SEED was founded, two other, similar boarding schools opened in Massachusetts and New Jersey. Both schools closed due to lack of funding. Eric A. and Raj understood that a boarding school would require more money per student than what the government provided, but they did not want to depend fully on private fundraising. So they lobbied the federal and D.C. governments, successfully acquiring a boarding stipend in addition to the existing school funding provisions. As a result of their efforts, Washington, D.C., became the only city in the country with this particular legal provision, a key factor in helping SEED succeed as a sustainable model. Eric A. and Raj also negotiated a $14.2 million loan for the renovation and construction of its first campus. Over the course of eighteen months, they raised a total of $26 million for capital and start-up costs for SEED's first boarding school.

> "It's thrilling to have found a way to test our model while living out our dream."
> —Eric Adler

In 1998, the first SEED School opened in Anacostia, one of the most distressed neighborhoods in Washington, D.C., and the entire country. The first class consisted of forty seventh graders, the majority of whom were two grade levels behind and lived below the poverty line in single-parent households. Today, the school is at capacity, with 320 students in grades seven through twelve. This model of public boarding-

school education has proven to be quite effective. Compared to their public-school peers, SEED students score higher on standardized tests, have better self-esteem, and are less likely to use drugs. The SEED School was one of only two non-selective public schools in Washington, D.C., to meet the federal government's "No Child Left Behind" academic standards in 2005. Ninety-seven percent of SEED School graduates continue on to four-year colleges, compared to 45 percent of their public-school peers. Graduates of SEED are attending schools such as American, Georgetown, University of Pennsylvania, Ohio Wesleyan, Princeton, Howard, and North Carolina A&T.

Eric A. has found the satisfaction he sought early in his career by asking tough questions about the way things work and daring to propose a new way. He challenged himself to figure out what it would take to provide quality education to disadvantaged children in our nation's urban public schools. When he did not see a satisfactory model for achieving this goal, he invented one, in true entrepreneurial fashion.

A bold and meaningful career in the nonprofit sector requires both continuous learning and continuous questioning. Curiosity feeds your creativity and takes you in interesting new directions. "Waking up in the morning with fifteen things to do and knowing how to do only eight of them is, to me, the definition of *new and untested*," Eric A. says. "If you don't know how to do everything, you'll learn. You don't have to know everything in advance. If you did, you'd never be able to do anything."

"There are great after-school programs. There are great mentoring programs. There are great scholarship programs, drama programs, and tutoring programs. The SEED School is all that, all the time."

—Eric Adler

In other words, being comfortable with uncertainty and embracing adventure are important qualities for those reaching for that next *new and untested* idea.

Getting to Impact

Raj's grandfather, a farmer in India, earned only thirty rupees a month (less than one American dollar). Still, he managed to send six children, including Raj's father, to college. Education was very important in Raj's household—priority one, two, *and* three. Raj was taught early on that education was the key not only to a good job, but also to upward mobility and lasting success for the entire family. Raj majored in molecular biology at Princeton University and landed a job as a management consultant after graduation. Many of the research and analytical skills he had acquired while studying the sciences proved applicable to his consulting work.

Discovering a new and untested idea involves combining rigorous research with rigorous dreaming.

Yet Raj was essentially living two lives. After contending with the pressures of his day job, he spent most evenings poring over articles, reports, and current research outlining the state of the American public school system. The opportunities available to Raj, because of his access to high-quality education, were denied to millions of kids around the country, especially in the inner city and in failing public schools. He was consumed by the question of how to reduce the inequities in the American educational system. Like Eric A., Raj became convinced that public boarding school education was one answer for low-income students.

> "To be entrepreneurial is to want to get up in the morning and face an overwhelming number of challenges and see them as opportunities."
> —Raj Vinnakota

Life is a series of choices. At some point, we choose how much and in what way we will contribute to the causes that matter to us. Raj made the choice to invest more and care more. After three years as a management consultant, he took a leave to research the feasibility of public boarding-school education.

For two months, he traveled around the country to understand more fully the urban education landscape. He studied existing boarding school models; talked to teachers, principals, educational administrators, and other experts; and discussed financial models for education with investors. He spent time in cities across the country, meeting as many people as possible who were open to the idea.

Being Bold is seeking answers.

Very few people, however, saw the possibility for an urban public boarding school. Most did not believe that the challenging logistical issues—developing sustainable funding levels, acquiring land or facilities, locking in local community support—could be overcome. Despite the skepticism he encountered, Raj pressed forward. His research and his belief in the concept made him certain that his idea could work. By the end of 1996, he had organized hundreds of pages of his findings and ideas and sent them to fifteen people he had met during his travels, including Eric Adler.

Discipline and strategic thinking turn a *new and untested* idea into concrete action.

Creating a *new and untested* idea is one thing. Transforming that idea into a tangible product, service, or program is another. That transformation is the difference between potential and true impact. Urban boarding schools sounded promising to Eric A. and Raj, but to establish one successfully, they had to develop a model that would fulfill their social vision and be financially viable. They knew that they had to follow up on their innovative thinking with careful research, planning, and implementation. "You've got to do everything with an eye toward outcomes," Eric A. says. "There are limited resources in this world to work on the things we're working on, and they've got to be invested effectively." Innovative ideas are only as good as their execution—and the success of the execution is measured by the outcome achieved.

Raj says that he and Eric A. are "absolutely crazy" about details when they make strategic decisions. They view an issue from every imaginable vantage point, carefully considering the consequences of each step. "We tree-diagram," Raj says. "If we say 'yes' to this, where does that go? If we say 'no' to this, what does that mean? To whom? What would someone else say? We work all the way through it. Then we can make the best decision based on that set of choices and parameters." Raj and Eric A. generate the best results possible by thinking big and then paying attention to tiny details.

"A lot of people spend too much time on the idea and not enough time on the execution. If you have a spectacular, brand-new idea and execute it badly, it will not fly. Execution is vital."
—Raj Vinnakota

Reframing Risk

Two months after Raj and Eric A. met, they had both quit their jobs and started working full-time on The SEED School while living off their savings. With no guarantee of success, they leaped from high-paying, secure consulting jobs to entrepreneurship in the nonprofit sector. By any definition, what they were doing was risky.

Yet Raj and Eric A. reframed the notion of risk. They decided that doing nothing was riskier than failing to pursue their vision—riskier for themselves and for the children they wished to serve. Taking a chance was part of discovering their potential. Raj never wanted to look

back on his life and think, *I did not take this risk, this opportunity to try an idea that I really believed in.* Raj and Eric A. also had the advantage of youth; they were unencumbered enough to give their all to SEED.

New and untested means redefining risk as opportunity.

If accepting risk means taking a leap of faith, risk management means staying the course. Raj and Eric A. could not guarantee The SEED School's success, even though they believed that it would succeed. But they could create optimal conditions for success by forming a solid strategic plan, building a strong, disciplined team, and understanding thoroughly the issue of public boarding-school education.

Raj calls himself and Eric A. the most "risk-averse risk takers" he knows. Even though they take many chances, they never do so without first deliberating and doing significant research. "Nothing successful is going to get done without some measure of risk," Eric A. says. "However, you've got to calculate and weigh the merits of those risks carefully, then take the ones that are worth taking and move on."

If you have ever pursued a goal, an idea, or a cause about which you cared passionately, you too had to reframe the definition of risk. You performed a mental calculation and decided that the opportunity to work for something meaningful outweighed the resistance or challenges you would face.

Embracing New and Untested Qualities

True innovation is as uncommon as it is powerful. The stories of MDRI and SEED show us how a new idea can become reality. Eric Rosenthal, Eric Adler, and Raj Vinnakota show us ways to be creative, imaginative and successful in the nonprofit sector. They have the qualities needed to make an impact in their fields: curiosity, creativity, passion, courage, discipline, drive, resolve, entrepreneurial zeal, the willingness to take risks, and the ability to balance patience and impatience. These qualities make up a recipe for boldness.

If you have a groundbreaking idea for social change, whether for a new organization, a program, or a strategy within your existing organization, marshal all of your internal and external resources to build and test that idea. If you are committed to pursuing a fulfilling career in the nonprofit sector, strive to embody the qualities demonstrated by Eric R., Eric A., and Raj, and allow those qualities to shape you professionally and personally. It comes down to deciding how you show up in the world. If the answer is *boldly*, get ready, because you will make a staggering impact.

Consider This

- At which activities do you excel? What skills come naturally to you? What do your friends and family identify as your strengths and skills?

- Are you a risk taker? Identify at least three instances in which you took a big chance on something or someone. What gave you the courage to take these risks?

- Do you ever question the way things work or the status quo? Do you ever wonder why things are done in a certain way and imagine how they might be done differently and better? Think of at least two issues or problems in your community. Why do you think these problems exist? What are the current approaches taken to alleviate these problems? Can you identify a different way to attack these problems?

- Are there topics or subjects about which you know a lot and can talk knowledgeably? Are there issues that capture your attention or interest?

- Think of three of your most creative or original ideas. Did you pursue them? If not, why not? As you revisit these ideas, how might you go about making them a reality?

Be Bold

City Year corps members engaged in a physical service project

Katie Redford, Echoing Green Fellow, in Washington, D.C.

Chapter Four

Seeing Possibilities

Your Hope Journey

Hope is a stunningly powerful force. It drives us to reach further than we thought possible and to persevere despite uncertainty and challenges. The nonprofit sector is an industry built on hope: hope for the future and hope for a better world. Your own desire to find a fulfilling career likely comes, in part, from the hope of living a life of meaning and significance. So how do you make hope actionable and turn it into a vision for your life and your work?

Finding your personal vision takes time. The first step is opening yourself up to various experiences and learning something from all of them, good and bad. If you use your experiences to develop wisdom and self-knowledge, you will begin to understand your place in the world and *see possibilities* for your future. Those bold enough to take this vision to the next level will also begin to *see possibilities* for the future of others. They will look at the world as it is and imagine the world as it might be.

You will try to eliminate problems instead of living with them. You will challenge the status quo instead of accepting it. It's about reframing a challenge as an opportunity. It's about taking your desire to work for the greater good and opening your mind to envision change. This fresh way of thinking is visionary and even revolutionary. Boldly *seeing possibilities* will direct you toward your personal vision for change.

Striving to fulfill your vision requires patience and perseverance. But if you commit to it, your vision will fuel you, sustain you, and give you the potential to spark great change. *Seeing possibilities* puts you ahead of the curve: You may spot opportunities for change long before others can understand or accept them. You will encounter obstacles. Welcome these tests as an opportunity to deepen and refine your thinking and stand firm for what you believe. This is your own journey of hope.

Slaying Giants

While growing up in Wellesley, Massachusetts, and attending college at Colgate University, Katie Redford was a competitive athlete. In addition to joining both the swim team and the diving team, she played Division I rugby. A grinder, she played as hard as she worked. When Katie graduated from college in 1990, she knew that she wanted to become a lawyer. But before settling in for three years of law school, she wanted to see the world. She joined WorldTeach and taught English in a small village along the border of Thailand and Burma.

What Katie experienced there changed her life forever. The AIDS epidemic in Thailand was at its height. Katie heard about the excessive logging in nearby jungles that was devastating the local environment. And she saw, up close, the impact of Burma's brutal military dictatorship as the military and opposition rebels battled along the border. Scores of Burmese were streaming into Thailand to escape the armed conflict. In acknowledgment of these realities, Katie included AIDS education and environmental awareness in her English classes. She also decided to learn more about the refugee situation along the border. During her summer break, she headed for a Thai refugee camp to live with a displaced Burmese family and teach English.

Being Bold is seeing possibilities in difficult circumstances.

Katie taught in a bamboo hut against a backdrop of exploding bombs and raging fights between the Burmese military and pro-democracy forces. She spent most of her time listening to refugees' horrific tales of the murder, rape, forced labor, and torture they endured as they desperately tried to escape Burma's military dictatorship. As the violence escalated, the Burmese refugees began to look to Katie and other foreign relief

workers for additional help. They told their stories to anyone who would listen.

One plea made to Katie has always stayed with her: "Use your freedom to promote ours. Please don't forget about us." This was more than she had signed on for—but she could not turn away. The unspeakable horror and tragedy formed a bond between these refugees and Katie. Her experience in the refugee camp was her *moment of obligation*. She would spend the next three years preparing to honor her promise.

Because she believed in the power of the law to protect and serve, Katie enrolled at the University of Virginia Law School in the fall of 1992. She acquired her legal education through her law school classes but also through her frequent trips back to the Thai-Burmese border. While studying human rights law and environmental law, she started a human rights group at the law school. After her second year, she received a fellowship to study the World Bank's work in Thailand and Burma, which would help her better understand the impact of global institutions on a country's development.

While overseas, Katie took a number of risks to document the many human rights abuses suffered by Burmese refugees. A pro-democracy activist arranged to sneak her into Burma to record abuses by the military associated with the construction of the Yadana Pipeline in the jungles of Burma. This billion-dollar oil pipeline was a project of the French company Total and the California-based Unocal, one of the last American companies doing business in Burma. Katie spent weeks on a boat going up and down the Salween River near the border to interview refugees. She found that women had been raped by members of the military. Families were forced from their homes at gunpoint and relocated to make way for the pipeline. Villages were torched. One woman reported that the military had kicked her baby into the fire, killing him. Katie developed malaria during one of her trips, but she continued on nonetheless.

Katie noticed that while those she interviewed spoke emotionally about their personal suffering, they were just as emotional about the suffering of their lands. Excessive logging destroyed the jungles and wreaked havoc on local ecosystems. Projects like the Yadana Pipeline were displacing villagers from the lands of their ancestors. And unsustainable development trends were creating water supply shortages and killing the animals that villagers relied on for food. The refugees placed these environmental abuses on par with the human rights abuses they had experienced.

"When I asked the Burmese people about human rights issues, they talked about forced labor, rape, and torture—but they also talked about losing their land. I realized that the connection between human rights and environmental rights was real."

—Katie Redford

Back at law school, Katie spent a lot of time processing what she had seen in the field. She realized how much of her work existed at the intersection of two distinct fields: human rights and environmental protection. She began to envision ways to bring together the tools and resources of both fields in new and powerful ways. She found a kindred spirit in her law school classmate Tyler Giannini, and the two of them began to explore what this *new and untested* territory might look like.

"I saw myself as someone who'd do human rights professionally and care about the environment in my personal life. But then I realized that this separation between the fields was not the way reality is in most of the world."

—Katie Redford

During their final year of law school, Katie and Tyler began to zero in on Unocal's role in the human rights abuses of Burmese villagers affected by the Yadana Pipeline. They were looking for a way to hold this U.S. corporation accountable. After some independent research, they decided to focus on the Alien Torts Claims Act, a little-used law dating from 1789. It allowed citizens of other countries to sue in U.S. courts for human rights violations occurring overseas. Their intuition told them that they were on to something big.

Katie wrote a paper called "Corporate Accountability for Human Rights Abuses Under the Alien Tort Claims Act: Unocal in Burma, a Case Study." The paper detailed the way the Alien Torts Claims Act should be used to sue Unocal for the human rights abuses connected to the pipeline. Although Katie received an A on the paper, her professor dismissed her proposal as totally unrealistic. He thought that Katie was naive and that her approach would never pass muster in a court of law. He further believed that international human rights issues had no place in the U.S. courts. Undeterred by this negative feedback, Katie held firm in her belief that no one had sued Unocal yet simply because no one fully understood the horror of the situation. She could *see possibilities* where so many could not.

Seeing possibilities means persevering through uphill battles.

After graduating from law school in 1995, Katie received seed money from Echoing Green to launch EarthRights International (ERI) with Tyler and Ka Hsaw Wa, a human rights activist from the Karen ethnic group, one of Burma's main ethnic nationalities. Working from offices in Thailand and Washington, D.C., they launched ERI as a nonprofit organization that combines the power of law and the power of people in defense of human rights and the environment. Working at the intersection of human rights and the environment—an intersection they define as "earth rights"—ERI specializes in documenting abuses, mounting legal actions against perpetrators of earth rights abuses, providing training for grassroots and community leaders, and launching advocacy campaigns. The day after the bar exam, Katie packed up and moved to Thailand to run ERI and prepare the lawsuit against Unocal. Her move marked the beginning of a decade-long battle that would test her patience but never her belief that she was on the side of justice.

"We saw horrific human rights abuses, this American oil company involved and benefiting, and we believed that there was no way we would lose once we exposed this."

—Katie Redford

EarthRights International brought the case of *John Doe I, et al., v. Unocal Corp., et al.*, to state and federal courts in California. Most legal experts said flatly that the case would never fly. Although ERI watched their case get dismissed in 2000, they fought back and won, on appeal, the right to continue.

After ERI's countless hours of legal work, Unocal agreed to settle the lawsuit in 2005. It was the first time in history that a major multinational corporation had settled a case of this type for monetary damages. In the landmark settlement, the company agreed to compensate the Burmese villagers who sued the firm for complicity in forced labor, rape, and murder.

Seeing possibilities means making your work personal.

Just as important as the monetary settlement is the strong legal precedent set by the Unocal case. As a result of ERI's efforts, a series of rulings in the California federal court established that a corporation can be held liable in U.S. courts for encouraging human rights violations by a foreign government. This puts corporations on notice and forces them to consider the legal and financial ramifications of their actions abroad. EarthRights International continues to use the Unocal case as a model to pursue similar lawsuits in other countries around the world, such as Nigeria and India.

To remain committed in the face of great odds, you must find a way to stay connected to the heart of the issue you are confronting. For Katie, the Unocal case was not just an academic or a legal success. Rather, it mattered on a personal level to people she cared deeply about. She says, "It's one thing to say you're committed to human rights. But if you say, 'If I fail, this mother whose baby was kicked into a fire is going to lose her case,' your commitment becomes much more urgent." *Seeing possibilities* for justice allowed Katie to ignore the odds and focus on the people who would benefit from her vision rather than on the people who were opposing her vision.

EarthRights International played the David to Unocal's Goliath. It continues to slay giants in its quest to protect human rights and the environment. ERI opened two schools in Ecuador and Thailand as a way of empowering indigenous people to protect their rights. ERI has also started a grassroots education and outreach campaign in the United States to teach the American public about the law's power to protect ordinary citizens. The legal expertise of ERI is so sought-after that it often has to turn down cases. Its work has been recognized in countless articles, documentaries, and even songs. It has received many awards, including the Goldman Prize (the world's most prestigious environmental prize), the Reebok Human Rights Award, and the Sting and Trudie Styler Award for Human Rights and the Environment.

"What is our risk of failure compared to people who are enduring the abuses and threats to their very survival? How could we not do this?"
—Katie Redford

Katie's vision for change has fueled and sustained her. *Seeing possibilities* put her ahead of the curve. Although she encountered obstacles and roadblocks, she welcomed these tests as an opportunity to deepen her thinking and strengthen her resolve. This was her own journey of hope.

The Power of Young People

"**B**allerina or mathematician," Carolyn Laub used to say when describing her dream career. Her father was a mathematician, and on Saturday afternoons, he and Carolyn often worked on math problems at the kitchen table in their home in Santa Barbara, California.

Being Bold is refusing to be confined by expectations or labels.

Carolyn excelled in her math classes, but over time, she began to receive the message in school that math was a "boy's subject." "My dad helped me understand that I could prove the teachers and other students wrong," Carolyn says. "I was an example contrary to the stereotype. The idea empowered me." This experience helped her grow up with a strong sense that stereotypes are damaging and that it's important to defy them.

In college, Carolyn began to question her sexual orientation. Coming out is never easy for a young person, but Carolyn was lucky to have generally supportive parents, extended family, and friends. She knew many less-fortunate young people. Some were terrified to talk to their parents for fear of rejection, and others had been ostracized by family and friends after telling the truth. Carolyn understood that her process of coming out had been relatively easy because of the support she received, and she wanted to create similar positive experiences for others like her. Two years after graduating from college in 1995, Carolyn started a support group for lesbian, gay, bisexual, and transgender (LGBT) youth in the California Bay Area.

Carolyn found her work with LGBT youth incredibly rewarding. Her own journey enabled her to connect with the young people in personal ways. Many of them shared painful stories about the discrimination they faced in their schools because of their sexual orientation or gender identity. The members of the support group tried to develop ways to cope with these situations. But over time, Carolyn became increasingly frustrated as the stories of discrimination in schools accumulated. She realized that in order for this discrimination to end, the focus had to shift to reforming the schools themselves. This realization marked her switch from a service-based approach to a systems-based approach. It also marked a turning point in Carolyn's career as a youth activist committed to social change.

"Early on, I learned that I can change not just individual stereotypes but the very systems that discriminate against people."
—Carolyn Laub

Carolyn connected with other activists intent on mobilizing students, educating and lobbying state legislators about what was happening in schools, and proposing California state legislation to provide nondiscrimination protection for students. She was impressed by the strong level of student involvement with the issue. As a result of their activism, the state passed AB 537, the groundbreaking California Student Safety and Violence Prevention Act of 2000, which protects students from discrimination based on actual and perceived sexual orientation, gender identity, and gender expression. The legislation gave students and activists a framework around which to build a case for cultural and institutional change in schools.

Seeing possibilities means learning from all experiences, both positive and negative.

Gay-Straight Alliance (GSA) clubs, which have been forming in schools around the country since the late 1990s, serve as safe havens for LGBT youth and their straight allies and mobilize young people to push for safer and more tolerant conditions in schools. In 1998, as a result of coaching a young woman who had started a GSA club, Carolyn began *seeing possibilities*. She realized GSA clubs could be an important vehicle for student activism and positive social change in schools. Carolyn decided to create an infrastructure-building organization that would provide support and resources to all students starting and running GSA clubs around California. With seed funding and support from Echoing Green, Carolyn created the GSA Network later that year in San Francisco.

> "I was inspired to see that young people themselves were the leaders and activists, driven by their instincts to create change in their lives."
>
> —Carolyn Laub

Carolyn's work is deeply rooted in her belief that young people have the power to shape their world. Youth leadership development and empowerment lie at the heart of the GSA Network's mission. Young people play important leadership roles in the Network, serving on its regional Youth Councils and board of directors, making decisions about the organization's budget and development. The GSA Network's core progressive values are constantly reinforced and are used to further develop the next generation of caring, ethical leaders.

Seeing possibilities means staying true to your vision.

In 2001, the GSA Network faced a real test. In the Visalia school district in California, a gay male high-school student was consistently harassed by a teacher for wearing an earring. The teacher said to him, "Only two kinds of guys wear earrings: pirates and faggots. And I don't see any water around here." The student complained to the school, but the administration did nothing. The student and the GSA Network, represented by the American Civil Liberties Union (ACLU) of Northern California, sued the school district and settled the case successfully.

Seeing possibilities includes being able to show those possibilities to others.

The settlement agreement required the school district to conduct mandatory training for school administrators, teachers, and staff, kindergarten through twelfth grade, every year for three years; to set up appropriate systems for filing harassment complaints; and to provide mandatory anti-homophobia education for all ninth graders—education that GSA Network was subsequently contracted to provide. "We had been the adversaries, and then we became the partner that was actually helping the school district to improve the school climate," Carolyn says. "I'm very proud of how we took a negative situation and turned it into an opportunity for positive impact."

The case has become the model for settlement agreements in several other anti-LGBT student harassment cases that have been litigated in California and other states.

"Sometimes you find allies in places you would never have expected."

—Carolyn Laub

Seeing possibilities has helped Carolyn succeed in her work promoting school safety, non-discrimination, and youth activism. When GSA Network began in 1998, approximately forty GSA clubs existed in California, primarily in the San Francisco Bay Area. There are now more than 540 clubs. A full 40 percent of California high schools have GSA clubs, making it the state with the highest percentage of public schools with GSA clubs. Such exponential growth of GSA clubs and youth engagement in California schools is a mathematical manifestation of Carolyn's vision. Her plan is as expansive as it is inclusive, and as she receives feedback from students in other states, she sees possibilities for nationwide change. Carolyn says, "When I was in high school—only a little more than fifteen years ago—the idea of coming out or having a club like a GSA at school was unfathomable. But today, a national student movement is under way. Change is happening."

"I know how much life can change once you see all the possibilities there are for making a difference."

—Carolyn Laub

mesmerized by the lives and work of such figures as Harriet Tubman, Eli Whitney, and Sitting Bull.

Maya loved science, and from a young age she planned to become a medical doctor. She published her first scientific paper when she was fifteen years old. As a senior in high school, she was honored in the prestigious Westinghouse Science Talent Search. Maya majored in biology with a concentration in neuroscience at Bryn Mawr College, where she worked in a developmental neurobiology laboratory. After graduation, Maya won a Rotary Fellowship to travel throughout Southeast and South Asia. The trip was intended to be a one-year educational opportunity before she started medical school.

A Global Vision for Children

Maya Ajmera grew up in eastern North Carolina, where her father, who had emigrated from India, taught physics at the local university. She learned to navigate several worlds: a traditional Indian household, a diverse community typical of university towns, and a southern culture still burdened by deep racial tensions and historical wounds. In an area still seen through a black-or-white lens, Maya's South-Asian identity made her an outsider. The town library became her oasis, and she devoured its contents. Partial to historical biographies, she found herself

"I was one of those typical kids who was supposed to become a doctor. You never know what life has in store for you."
—Maya Ajmera

Having spent many summers with relatives in India while growing up, Maya felt at home traveling through the developing world. In all of her visits, she was struck by the hundreds of children she saw who were trying to navigate the world alone. Some were homeless; others were abandoned. During her year on a Rotary Fellowship, Maya was deeply moved by the grassroots organizations working to improve these children's lives. One encounter proved pivotal in redirecting Maya's path.

Being Bold means being open to and learning from new experiences.

While waiting for a train in Bhubaneshwar, the capital of the Indian state Orissa, Maya saw a group of children sitting on the train platform, listening intently to a woman who was teaching them. Intrigued, Maya approached the woman and asked what the children were doing. She learned that they were students in the Train Platform School, an organization that served some of the city's most impoverished children. Because they were living and working on train platforms in and around Bhubaneshwar, they could not attend school, so this program brought skills-based schooling to the children.

Maya was amazed by the power and effectiveness of this idea. She learned that a local schoolteacher, Inderjit Khurana, had started the program.

Maya also learned that it cost only about $600 a year to run a school with two teachers for forty children. She saw firsthand how small amounts of money in the developing world could create extraordinary improvements in children's lives. This was Maya's *moment of obligation*. She knew that her life's mission involved working with programs like the Train Platform Schools; she just needed to figure out exactly what her involvement would be.

When Maya returned to the United States, she broke the news to her parents that she would put off medical school. Instead, she enrolled at Duke University's Terry Sanford Institute for Public Policy to study international development and economics.

The scope of global child poverty is staggering. Around the world, more than 300 million children and youth live in desperate straits. Most of these impoverished children are girls, and half of them are illiterate. The majority work to support themselves or their families, so they cannot attend school. Largely invisible and ignored, these children suffer partly because of the way foreign aid is structured. Governments and large institutions distribute hundreds of millions of dollars each year to developing countries for economic development, infrastructure projects, and humanitarian assistance. Yet very little of this aid trickles down to the world's neediest and poorest children, whom Maya refers to as "children of the last mile."

Maya began *seeing possibilities* for something powerful. Sometimes the questions asked are more important than the answers generated. Questioning and probing sends you past accepted ideas and allows you to envision a new, better solution. She was awash in questions: Why can't we distribute foreign aid in more targeted and effective ways? Why would foreign aid flow to large institutions with no connection to those most in need rather than to community-based organizations with a better understanding of the local situation? Why can't we channel small amounts of money to grassroots organizations doing amazing work in developing countries with young people whom society has forgotten?

Seeing possibilities starts with asking hard questions.

In 1994, after winning a seed grant from Echoing Green, Maya set out to build a new type of global institution: The Global Fund for Children (GFC). GFC is a grant-making organization that invests in some of the best community-based organizations around the world that serve the most vulnerable children and youth. GFC awarded a first grant of $3,000. Since that time, the organization has awarded over $6 million to more than 200 organizations in sixty countries around the world. The programs supported by GFC touch tens of thousands of children. GFC's model shows that small investments can have a huge impact.

"The ultimate goal of GFC ultimately is to advance the dignity of children and youth around the world."
—Maya Ajmera

The Global Fund for Children also harnesses the power of books, films, and documentary photography to advance the dignity of children and youth. This social enterprise component helps GFC to support a portion of its grantmaking program. In 1994, Maya set out to publish her first book, *Children from Australia to Zimbabwe*. It highlights how young people live in twenty-six countries, one for each letter of the alphabet. The book was rejected by every publisher in New York. Publishers thought that Maya was too young for such a project, that her lack of a track record in the children's book-publishing world made her book unmarketable, and that the book had no commercial appeal.

Seeing possibilities means moving past rejection.

So Maya decided to publish the book herself. She says, "That's what social entrepreneurs do—if you can't find someone to do it, you do it yourself." In 1996, *Children from Australia to Zimbabwe* was released. Maya donated three copies to every public school in North Carolina. She turned over the remaining copies to a commercial book distributor in North Carolina.

Within four months, every book had been sold and it went on to win many awards. GFC has now published twenty books. More than 350,000 copies are currently in circulation with families, libraries, and schools around the world, with an estimated readership of about 1 million readers. The books, a tribute to the critical role reading played in Maya's own life, help her share her vision. Maya hopes that The Global Fund for Children Books will help young readers become caring global citizens and will remind us all that the children of the last mile are our children, too.

"Our books are the soul of what we want to tell the world—this is who children are and what they can be."
—Maya Ajmera

It's hard not to take rejection personally or let it shake your confidence. It stings and can make you question yourself. But it is crucial to do as Maya did: push through uncertainty and persevere. To Maya, a publisher's rejection letter did not cast the worth of her book into doubt; rather, it showed that the publisher simply did not share her vision. Maya's hope for a better life for the world's most vulnerable continues to drive her. By reaching out to others who share her commitment, she is creating a collective vision for global change.

"This work is a fight against global poverty. I feel like I have a moral imperative to do what I can to help."
—Maya Ajmera

Crafting your Personal Vision

It's probably good advice not to take yourself too seriously. At the same time, though, creating a career with impact requires careful thought and deliberation. If you are searching for your place in the world or trying to determine your life path, commit to the journey, wherever it may lead.

Katie Redford, Carolyn Laub, and Maya Ajmera didn't have any answers when their journeys began. But they did possess a willingness to be open to and influenced by different experiences, and they had the imagination to envision a different world for themselves and others. They could *see possibilities* where others couldn't. Honor your imagination by following it without fear. It is challenging you to create your own personal dreams for a better world.

Consider This

- Are there social issues or problems that trouble you? Are you pessimistic about them or do you have hope that things might change for the better one day? If you are hopeful, how do you think things might change? What can you do to make things change?

- Are there experiences or opportunities that you have always wanted to take advantage of but haven't? Why haven't you? What had you hoped to get out of these experiences?

- How do you engage in learning in your life? From what sources do you get new ideas and perspectives?

- Are you afraid of conflict? How do you react when others challenge you or disagree with you? Is it important to you that most people agree with you or take your side?

- Think of an experience during which you pushed on despite difficulties and challenges. What allowed you to be resilient? Where did your motivation come from?

Be Bold

Students in a Teach For America classroom

Chapter Five

Bold as a Career Choice

Time to Be Bold

We hope that the stories of the Echoing Green Fellows profiled in *Be Bold* hold some meaning and spark in you a desire to begin or further develop an exciting and meaningful career in the nonprofit sector. Working in the nonprofit sector means that you have made a commitment to seeking positive change in the world and to developing the tools and skills that will make this happen. From those who made dramatic career changes to pursue something more meaningful to those who take on tough issues despite the odds against them, the people profiled in *Be Bold* prove that there is no one path to your goal. There is only *your* way. However different the trajectories of the Echoing Green Fellows have been, all of them have gone about their journeys boldly. They have followed what's called them, confronted fear and moved beyond it, developed a personal vision for the way things could be in this world, and used their creativity to bring their visions to life.

Use their stories to create your own action plan for boldness. A moment of obligation challenges you to take responsibility for and commit to an issue that may seem overwhelming and difficult at first. The gall to think big allows you to ignore others' expectations and to create big solutions to vexing social problems. Pursuing new and untested ideas means thinking creatively and dreaming up new solutions to old problems. And finally, seeing possibilities means spotting opportunities before others and then enacting your unique vision for a better world.

Being Bold professionally in the nonprofit sector means fighting for change, standing up to what's wrong, and thinking creatively about how to make things right. **Being Bold** in your personal life means developing such a high level of self-awareness, self-knowledge, and self-mastery that you become your own best self. There truly is nothing more powerful than that! You link the two kinds of boldness by developing a vision for your unique place in the world and acting on it.

We suggest that you take the time to think about and answer the questions that are listed in the following pages. This process will help you get to know yourself better and identify ways in which you are already **Being Bold**. You can use this knowledge to develop a new, powerful direction for yourself.

The First Step: Finding Your Truest Self

Truly getting to know yourself is a challenging (and lifelong) process. One of the most powerful ways to jump-start this effort, especially while you are young, is to take risks and test yourself, being aware of what works, what feels right, and what doesn't. Asking a lot of questions of yourself is a wonderful way to understand and check in with yourself. For example, "What excites me? What are my particular talents? What lessons did I learn from that experience?"

Being reflective requires you to analyze your motives and actions, strategize and plan your next steps, and seek honest input and feedback from peers, family members, and mentors. It's an intense process but a worthwhile one. Reflection can reveal what makes you happy, help you understand how you see yourself, and allow you to envision your place in the world.

To get started, answer the following:

1. **What does your "hair down/shoes off" self look like? What are you doing during these moments?**

_____

_____

_____

_____

_____

_____

_____

_____

_____

_____

2. What actions have you taken in your life that best reflect what's meaningful to you? Why were they meaningful?

_____

_____

_____

_____

_____

_____

3. What do you do that makes you feel most alive?

_____

_____

_____

_____

_____

4. If you had one word tattooed on your body, what would it be and why?

_____

_____

_____

_____

_____

Your Inspiration: Moment of Obligation

A *moment of obligation* entails committing to what means the most to you and accepting responsibility for your dreams. Whether you recognize it now or not, you have likely experienced *moments of obligation* but may have not acted on them.

No one can know better than you what you want, but too often, fear, pride, and the expectations of other people get in the way. Learn to trust yourself, your instincts, and your feelings as you begin to think about and navigate your career path. Answering these questions will help.

1. **What truly inspires you? What are you drawn toward? What moves you? Get very, very specific. (You can list a social issue, task, role, emotion, or something else.)**

_____

_____

_____

_____

_____

_____

2. **How do you know these things inspire/draw/move you? What happens?**

_____

_____

_____

_____

_____

_____

3. Whom have you learned the most from? Why are these people your most influential teachers? What have they taught you?

_____

_____

_____

_____

_____

_____

4. Trace the decisions you made in your life that have led you to where you are today.

_____

_____

_____

_____

_____

5. Now think about these decisions as possible _moments of obligation._ Does that change the way you see them? If so, in what ways?

_____

_____

_____

_____

_____

_____

6. Describe your most significant *moment of obligation*. How do you know it was a *moment of obligation?*

_____

_____

_____

_____

_____

_____

7. As you think about a possible role for yourself in the nonprofit sector, think about what inspires/draws/moves you. How might that link to your career or your next job?

_____

_____

_____

_____

_____

Larger Than Life: Gall to Think Big

When you have the *gall to think big*, you aren't afraid to go for it. Big problems in the world don't scare you. Rather, they motivate you. You are confident, solution oriented, and strategic as you tackle large issues. You operate beyond others' expectations of you and rely on your own internal compass to drive you forward. Most important, you understand that you are part of something larger than yourself.

Answering these questions will help you think of your career as a way to take on big issues and problems about which you care deeply.

1. **Which social movements, from today or from any point in history, resonate the most with you? Why? Have you been involved in any work that you would define as part of a social movement?**

_____

_____

_____

_____

_____

_____

2. **If your career (in its entirety—think long term) allowed you to tackle a few big problems in the world (e.g., educational inequity, poverty), what would they be?**

_____

_____

_____

_____

_____

_____

3. As a change maker, write down your most ambitious goal. How would you begin achieving this goal?

_____

_____

_____

_____

_____

_____

4. What would the world look like if you achieved the goal laid out in question three?

_____

_____

_____

_____

_____

_____

5. How would your work impact your grandchildren?

_____

_____

_____

_____

_____

Finding Solutions: New and Untested

New and untested is the process of innovating for the greater good. It is coming up with new ideas, new strategies, and new methodologies to tackle and solve tough problems. This requires a great deal of courage, in part because your new approach may challenge the status quo. *New and untested* is a different way of thinking. It requires you to question the way things *are* and imagine the way things *could be*. Answering the following questions can help you draw on your ability to innovate and be creative.

1. **What are some of the most creative things you have done (could be anything— from a pottery project to organizing a rally)? What skills did you draw on to accomplish that creative thing?**

2. **What is the biggest risk you have ever taken? This could be doing something new, putting yourself out there, taking an unpopular stance, or anything else you define as a risk. Was it worth it? How did taking the risk make you feel? What was the result?**

3. Is risk taking something that you do on a daily, monthly, or yearly basis, or never?

_____

_____

_____

_____

_____

4. If you were to take more risks in your educational or professional career, what types of things would you do?

_____

_____

_____

_____

_____

5. What are a few issues in your community or our world that frustrate you? For example, maybe you don't understand why a certain system is so inefficient, or perhaps you wonder why something is the way it is when it could be so much better.

_____

_____

_____

_____

_____

6. **Choose one of the issues you identified in the last question and outline the current approaches being used to address it. Brainstorm one or two new ways you might go about attacking and even solving that problem.**

_____

_____

_____

_____

7. **This month, practice skepticism regularly. When you look at an issue or a problem, try to understand what's really going on and why things remain the way they are. Challenge yourself to ask "why" questions every day and see what you learn. Note how your approach to problems changes after you complete this exercise.**

_____

_____

_____

_____

Visioning: Seeing Possibilities

Seeing possibilities first requires that you not walk away from or past a problem. Once you are committed to working on that problem, use your imagination to create solutions and envision what a world free of that problem would look like. At its core, _seeing possibilities_ is about having hope and turning hope into action by developing your own personal vision of change in the world.

Work in the nonprofit sector can be very challenging. There is always more to be done. The tasks can seem endless and frustrating and the change incremental. But nonprofit work can also be exhilarating and fulfilling. It allows you to be involved in the important issues of the day and make a significant difference in the world. *Seeing possibilities* is the reason you get up every morning and the reason we all believe in a better tomorrow.

Here are some questions to explore.

1. **Look back at what you have written thus far. Now answer: What do you wish for yourself, your community (however you define it), and the world? Include your thoughts on your professional career.**

_____

_____

_____

_____

_____

2. **Lay out the steps you need to take in order to achieve your professional vision.**

_____

_____

_____

_____

_____

3. It takes most of us a lot of time to figure out what really captures our attention. Make a list of five experiences you will pursue in the next year to explore what your long-term focus might be.

_____

_____

_____

_____

_____

4. When historians write your biography, what do you want them to say about you? For what do you want to be remembered?

_____

_____

_____

_____

Dare to Live Boldly

The questions in this chapter are meant to help you uncover your hopes, dreams, and passions. These are the sources of your power. If you choose to own this power, just imagine what you can accomplish. Nothing is beyond your reach, not even the ability to change the world.

Complete these statements:

My *moment of obligation* **has led me to:**

_____

_____

_____

By acknowledging this *moment of obligation,* **I have the** *gall to think big* **about:**

_____

_____

_____

If I were to act on my *gall to think big* **and develop a** *new and untested idea,* **it would be:**

_____

_____

_____

If my *new and untested* **idea were fully enacted, I** *see possibilities* **that the world would be better in the following ways:**

_____

_____

_____

Come back to your words often. They are your bold plan for creating a better world.

Visit www.bebold.org to continue exploring.

PARTNERS & RESOURCES

Be Bold's Key Partners

AMERICAN HUMANICS
www.humanics.org
American Humanics is a national alliance of colleges, universities, and nonprofits dedicated to educating, preparing, and certifying professionals to lead and strengthen nonprofit organizations. Providing experiential education and innovative curricula that supply college and university students with the skills to become leaders in America's nonprofit organizations, American Humanics is a pioneering organization that is currently the only national nonprofit to meet this crucial need.

CITY YEAR
www.cityyear.org
City Year's mission is a is to build democracy through citizen service, civic leadership, and social entrepreneurship. City Year works toward the full realization of this vision through three core activities: running a full-time youth service corps; engaging citizens in service through large-scale, high-impact community events; and leading the discussion and development of national service policies and programs. City Year's objective is to provide excellent service in our communities and increase awareness and support for citizen service among leaders across the country and the world.

GOOD MAGAZINE
www.goodmagazine.com
Good Magazine is a high-impact consumer magazine that covers the people, ideas, and institutions driving change in the world. Combining relevance and entertainment, the magazine provides a cultural platform for those who want to do well by doing good. Its subscription campaign donates 100 percent of subscription revenue to twelve innovative nonprofit organizations, including City Year, Witness, and Teach For America. GOOD's mission is to stimulate the culture of good by creating dialogue around things that matter.

IDEALIST – ACTION WITHOUT BORDERS
www. idealist.org
Since 1995, Action Without Borders has connected hundreds of thousands of people with job, intern, and volunteer opportunities from over 56,000 organizations in the nonprofit sector through its website, Idealist. org. Idealist is the largest directory of nonprofit organizations on the web and also offers several comprehensive resource centers devoted to nonprofit

careers and management, including "Tools for Managers," "The Nonprofit Career Center," "Volunteering Abroad," and "Financial Management for Nonprofit Staff." In addition, Action Without Borders has hosted over 100 "Nonprofit Career" and "Graduate Degrees for the Public Good" fairs across the United States in partnership with various universities and nonprofit support organizations.

KELLOGG FOUNDATION
www.wkkf.org
The W. K. Kellogg Foundation was established in 1930 in order "to help people help themselves." Today, the organization is one of the world's largest private foundations with grants awarded in the United States, southern Africa, Latin America and the Caribbean, and focused on the four areas of health, food systems and rural development, youth and education, and philanthropy and volunteerism.

THE NEW YORK TIMES JOB MARKET
www.nytimes.com/jobs
Job Market, the print and online recruitment services of The New York Times, provides employers and job seekers with comprehensive resources to streamline the recruitment process. Job Market appears in *The New York Times* every Sunday and is updated throughout the week at nytimes.com, where job seekers can find job listings, career-related *Times* articles, exhaustive company research, a resume database, and valuable career resources. Through the newspaper's national audience, which includes 4.5 million weekday readers and 5.2 million Sunday readers as well as the 1.4 million average daily unique visitors to nytimes.com, The New York Times Job Market reaches a marketplace of high-quality professionals actively seeking new job opportunities or considering career moves.

PARTNERS & RESOURCES

These resources are good places to start as you are building a powerful career in the nonprofit sector.

denotes Be Bold key partners

NONPROFIT CAREER RESOURCES

Bridgestar
• www.bridgestar.org

Charity Village
• www.charityvillage.com

* Idealist.org
• www.idealist.org

* The New York Times Job Market
• www.nytimes/jobs

Opportunity Knocks
• www.opportunitynocs.org

CIVIC ENGAGEMENT AND PUBLIC SERVICE

Altrusa International, Inc.
• www.altrusa.com

AmeriCorps
• www.americorps.gov

Catholic Network of Volunteer Services
• www.cnvs.org

Center for Community Change
• www.communitychange.org

Hands on Network
• www.handsonnetwork.org

Jewish Coalition for Service
• www.jewishservice.org

National Peace Corps Association
• www.rpcv.org

Partnership for Public Service
• www.ourpublicservice.org

Points of Light Foundation
• www.pointsoflight.org

Public Allies
• www.publicallies.org

Youth Service America
• www.ysa.org

COLLEGIATE/GRADUATE NETWORKS

American Association of Community Colleges
• www.aacc.nche.edu

American Association of School Administrators
• www.aasa.org

Association of Professional Schools of International Affairs
• www.apsia.org

Campus Compact
• www.compact.org

National Association of Colleges and Employers
• www.naceweb.org

National Association of Schools of Public Affairs and Administration
• www.naspaa.org

Net Impact
• www.netimpact.org

FELLOWSHIP/SCHOLARSHIP PROGRAMS, FOUNDATIONS, AND FUNDING PROGRAMS

Ashoka
• www.ashoka.org

AVODAH
• www.avodah.net

Coro
• www.coro.org

Equal Justice Works
• www.equaljusticeworks.org

Humanity in Action Foundation
• www.humanityinaction.org

International Partnership for Service Learning and Leadership
• www.ipsl.org

New Profit
• www.newprofit.org

Posse Foundation
• www.possefoundation.org

Princeton Project 55
• www.project55.org

Public Policy and International Affairs Fellowship Program
• www.ppiaprogram.org

StartingBloc
• www.startingbloc.org

Strongheart Fellowship Program
• www.strongheartfellowship.org

UnLtd.
• www.unltd.org.uk

Watson Fellowship
• www.watsonfellowship.org

* W.K. Kellogg Foundation
• www.wkkf.org

Young People For Project
• www.youngpeoplefor.org

Youth Venture
• www.youthventure.org

LEADERSHIP DEVELOPMENT
* American Humanics
• www.humanics.org

Leader to Leader Institute
• www.leadertoleader.org

Leadership Learning Community
• www.leadershiplearning.org

Management Leadership for
Tomorrow
• www.ml4t.org

National Foundation for
Teaching Entrepreneurship
• www.nfte.com

MEDIA & WEBSITES
ChangeThis
• www.changethis.com

Chronicle of Philanthropy
• www.philanthropy.com

Daily Kos
• www.dailykos.com

Future Leaders in Philanthropy
(FLIP)
• www.flip.typepad.com/flip

* GOOD Magazine
• www.goodmagazine.com

MediaRights
• www.mediarights.org

MTVU
• www.mtvu.com

Nonprofit Online News
• www.news.gilbert.org

Ode Magazine
• www.odemagazine.com

Stanford Social Innovation
Review
• www.ssireview.org

WorldChanging.com
• www.worldchanging.com

YouthNoise
• www.youthnoise.com

NONPROFIT NETWORKS
85 Broads
• www.85broads.com

Council on Social Work
Education
• www.cswe.org

Craigslist Foundation
• www.craigslistfoundation.org

Emerging Practitioners in
Philanthropy
• www.epip.org

The Foundation Center
• www.fdncenter.org

Independent Sector
• www.independentsector.org

National Council of Nonprofit
Associations
• www.ncna.org

Network for Good
• www.networkforgood.org

Social Edge
• www.socialedge.org

Social Venture Network
• www.svn.org

Women's Funding Network
• www.wfnet.org

Working For Good
• www.workingforgood.com

Young Nonprofit Professionals
Network
• www.ynpn.org

YOUTH/STUDENT GROUPS
Campus Progress
• www.campusprogress.org

Global Justice
• www.globaljusticenow.org

Global Youth Action Network
• www.youthlink.org

Hillel
• www.hillel.org

The League of Young Voters
• www.indyvoter.org

National Society of Leadership and Success
• www.societyofsuccess.com

National Student Partnerships
• www.nspnet.org

NetAid
• www.netaid.org

Project 540
• www.gse.upenn.edu/cssc/project540

Student Environmental Action Coalition
• www.seac.org

Student Global AIDS Campaign
• www.fightglobalaids.org

Student Labor Action Project
• www.studentlabor.org

Summerbridge Breakthrough Alumni Network
• www.sbalumni.org

TakingITGlobal
• www.takingitglobal.org

United States Student Association
• www.usstudents.org

Echoing Green Fellows' Organizations Profiled in *Be Bold*
* City Year
• www.cityyear.org

EarthRights International
• www.earthrights.org

Free At Last
• www.freeatlast.org

Gay-Straight Alliance Network
• www.gsanetwork.org

The Global Fund For Children
• www.globalfundforchildren.org

International Bridges to Justice
• www.ibj.org

Mental Disability Rights International
• www.mdri.org

The SEED Foundation
• www.seedfoundation.com

Teach For America
• www.teachforamerica.com

Vision Youthz
• www.visionyouthz.org

World of Good
• www.worldofgood.com

Visit www.bebold.org for more information!